Learning Center Activities for the New Teacher

GRADE 1

by Maureen Betz

Illustrated by Gary Mohrman

Published by Frank Schaffer Publications
an imprint of

McGraw Hill Children's Publishing

Author: Maureen Betz

McGraw Hill Children's Publishing

Published by Frank Schaffer Publications
An imprint of McGraw-Hill Children's Publishing
Copyright © 2004 McGraw-Hill Children's Publishing

All Rights Reserved • Printed in the United States of America

Limited Reproduction Permission: Permission to duplicate these materials is limited to the person for whom they are purchased. Reproduction for an entire school or school district is unlawful and strictly prohibited.

Send all inquiries to:
McGraw-Hill Children's Publishing
3195 Wilson Drive NW
Grand Rapids, Michigan 49544

Learning Center Activities for the New Teacher—Grade 1
ISBN: 0-7682-2941-3

1 2 3 4 5 6 7 8 9 MAL 09 08 07 06 05 04
The **McGraw·Hill** Companies

Table of Contents

Introduction 1

Language Arts 3–34

    The Hope Window 3–6

    A Tea Party 7–10

    The Great Race 11–14

    Say It with Feeling 15–18

    May I Take a Message? 19–22

    Field of Friends 23–26

    Uncle John's Orchard 27–30

    The Vowel Game 31–34

Math 35–66

    The Celebration Calendar 35–38

    Geometry George and Jane 39–42

    Colorful Cottage 43–46

    Grandpa Elmer's Cupboard 47–50

    Critter Contest 51–54

    Shopping at the General Store 55–58

    Squirrel Sort 59–62

    How Many Tomatoes? 63–66

Science 67–94

    Insect Inventory 67–70

    What's in the Marsh? 71–74

    Exciting Electricity 75–78

    Jumping Germs! 79–82

    Treasures in the Soil 83–86

    How Old Are You? 87–90

    Wheels Make the World Go Round 91–94

Table of Contents, continued

Social Studies 95–118
- Log Cabin Days 95–98
- All in the Family 99–102
- A Few of My Favorites 103–106
- The Other Side 107–110
- What Did You Say? 111–114
- My Room 115–118

Music 119–130
- Lively Listening 119–122
- A Song by Me 123–126
- A Rainbow Rhyme 127–130

Art 131–138
- Glorious Glass 131–134
- Keepsake Memories 135–138

Appendix: The Shopping List 139–140

Introduction

What Is a Learning Center?

A classroom learning center is a student-focused, teacher-designed station for independent, experiential learning. Learning centers extend your lessons and allow students the thrill of discovery. Students are set for success with fun, engaging, interactive lessons.

In addition to cognitive skills, learning centers teach social skills. They build students' self-discipline and self-esteem. They promote independent, critical, and creative thinking. Students also can help plan or modify centers, giving them a sense of ownership.

Some centers require students to work in pairs or small groups, allowing them to practice cooperative skills and responsibility.

Standards

Learning centers support curriculum standards. The centers in this book are labeled with their correlating standards. Complete sets of standards and links to professional organizations that develop standards can be found at Education World, Inc.'s Web site, **www.educationworld.com/standards**. This book abbreviates the professional organizations like this: NCTE, National Council of Teachers of English; NCTM, National Council of Teachers of Mathematics; NAS, National Academies of Science; NCSS, National Council for the Social Studies; NSAE, National Standards for Art Education. Special areas within the discipline are listed before the standard number.

Organization

Adapt your classroom environment to allow for one or several centers. Centers should be separated enough from the main classroom area so that students in either place can concentrate on their tasks-at-hand. Centers can be used as review, reinforcement, or discovery. They should not be used for reward or punishment.

Introduce each center to your class. Give complete instructions and expectations. Show a sample or demonstration of what students are to do. Make the connection between the curriculum and the center obvious. When properly prepared, students will be better able to work independently and purposefully.

Allow at least 10 to 15 minutes a day for center time. Some centers will take longer than others. Some centers may span other projects or areas of inquiry. Some students will take longer in some centers than others. Be ready to be a "coach" to small groups and individuals during this time as you circulate around the room. Students not at centers will need to be on-task, too.

Keep your centers stored in labeled boxes and folders. You might include on the label the date you used the center, as well. Replace worn parts and replenish low supplies regularly. Students can help inventory materials. Plan ahead so that you can use centers year after year. Find ways to use materials for more than one center. Laminate pieces whenever possible to help preserve them.

Introduction, continued

Materials

The centers in this book use simple, easily-obtained materials. A complete list is found in the Appendix. Most materials are found at office supply or teacher supply stores, grocery stores, or at home. You will develop an eye for center materials as you shop thrift stores and garage sales, too. Apply the "KISS" principle to materials—"Keep It Simple and Safe."

Assessment

Much of center work is assessed on the honor system. At the beginning of the school year, develop and explain assessment expectations.

Generally, non-graded assessments are used in centers, with as much self-checking as possible. Responsibility for understanding falls to the student. You must provide a safe atmosphere for asking questions.

Assessments are given for each learning center in this book. In addition to self-check, assessments include making a class presentation, displaying work, evaluating others' work, and writing or orally reporting what the student learned.

Different record-keeping methods work for different people. To keep track of the progress of the class as a whole, use a wall chart with the name of the center and each student's name. The students will mark off their spaces when they finish the center. You can see at a glance who has done what.

Keep track of individual students by assigning a chart or folder to each and a designated place to keep them. The work that students put into their folders can be shown to parents during conferences.

Keep track of individual centers by placing a folder in the center in which students put their completed work.

Some teachers write contracts for each center, which both the teacher and student sign. In-and-out baskets and record books, either paper or on computer files, are other options. Develop a system that is simple and works for you.

How to Use This Book

Use the centers in this book as they are written, or use only the portions that appeal to you or fit your curriculum. Use the ideas here as a springboard for developing your own learning centers. Adapt what is here to suit your needs.

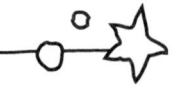

Language Arts　　　　　　　　　　　　　　　　　　　　*Standards Correlation*
　　　　　　　　　　　　　　　　　　　　　　　　　　　　NCTE 11, 12

The Hope Window

Introduction to the Learning Center

This center helps students build their vocabularies and heighten their abilities to express their personal values. Soft music and decorative art prints provide a soothing atmosphere for self-reflection.

Skills & Assessment

- Use words to express feelings
- Assess through individual discussion.

Tip

Make "The Hope Window" a regular part of your classroom environment. Select a poem of the month to display at the center and invite the students to write about the emotions they feel as they read the poem.

Language Arts   *The Hope Window, continued*

Teacher Materials

- several art prints
- comfortable child's chair
- small work table
- recordings of poetry and/or soothing music
- portable CD or tape player with earphones
- shoe box labeled "Hope Chest"

Student Materials

- reproducible pages 5 and 6
- colored pencils or markers
- glue

Teacher Directions

1. Copy pages 5 and 6 for each student. Cut up each *Word List* and put the word cards in the shoe box.
2. Set up and introduce the center. Tell the students that in this center they will think about the things that they hope for.
3. Select music and artwork for the center. Then give each student a copy of *My Hope Window* and explain the directions.

Student Directions

1. Look out the "Hope Window."
2. Think about what you hope for.
3. Look at the words in the Hope Chest.
4. Find a word or words that tell about something that is important to you. Glue the words onto your Hope Window.
5. Repeat until each windowpane has a word.
6. Color your Hope Window.

Extensions

Level Down

Ask a volunteer to work one-on-one with students who are reluctant to express their feelings.

Level Up

Give students an opportunity to write their own words in the windowpanes or create sentence poems that reflect their feelings.

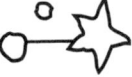

Name _____ Date _____

My Hope Window

Glue a hope word here.	Glue a hope word here.
Glue a hope word here.	Glue a hope word here.
Glue a hope word here.	Glue a hope word here.

The Hope Window, continued

Word List

friends	laughter	art
family	toys	good manners
good health	books	money
happiness	clothes	safety
awards	exercise	home
pets	fairness	school
love	music	
fun	sports	

Language Arts

Standards Correlation:
NCTE 3, 4, 5, 9, 12

A Tea Party

Introduction to the Learning Center

Tea parties are not just for *Alice in Wonderland*. This fun center turns a tea party into a full language arts experience, from writing an invitation to learning vocabulary and manners.

Skills & Assessment

- Develop social skills
- Reinforce vocabulary
- Assess by having students write thank-you notes using all the words in the search.

Tip

Expand this center by asking an adult volunteer to serve as a party consultant. Check with parents, local social organizations, catering services, or party organizers to locate volunteers.

Language Arts *A Tea Party, continued*

Teacher Materials

- self-adhesive notepads
- teapot
- four non-breakable place settings including plates, teacups and saucers, utensils, and napkins
- serving tray or plate
- lemonade or other beverage
- cookies or other appropriate food

Student Materials

- reproducible pages 9 and 10
- pencils

Teacher Directions

1. Group students into teams of four. Give each student an invitation (page 9) to complete for another member of his or her team.

2. Set up the center. Lay out the place settings, serving tray, and beverages.

3. Write each of the following words on a self-adhesive note: *cup, plate, pot, friends, fun.* Hide the notes under the dishes on the table.

4. Encourage the students to converse during the tea party.

5. Hand out reproducible page 10 and explain the directions after the students have finished their "tea." *Be sure to remove food and beverages from the table before the search begins.*

Student Directions

1. Invite someone from your team to a tea party. Fill out an invitation for him or her.

2. After your tea party, find hidden words around your table. Use the words to finish the sentences on your worksheet.

Extensions

Level Down

Complete the activity sentence by sentence, writing each search word on the board to assist students in finding a match.

Level Up

Hold a "bonus round" search for additional words. Have the students use the words in sentences.

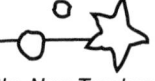

Name _____ Date _____

Invitation

A. Fill in the line on number 1 with the name of the person you are inviting.

B. Write the date of the party on line 2.

C. Write the time of the party on line 3.

D. Write your name on line 4.

E. Give the invitation to the person you invited.

---

1. Dear _____:

   Please come to my tea party.

2. Date: _____

3. Time: _____

   We will search for words. I hope you can attend.
   _____

   Very truly yours,

4.
   _____

Name _____   Date _____

Tea Party Search

Find the words hidden on the table to finish these sentences. Write the word on the blank line.

1. We drink tea from a _____.

2. Cookies are served on a _____.

3. The tea is in a _____.

4. We visit with _____.

5. The tea party is _____.

Language Arts

Standards Correlation:
NCTE 1, 2, 3, 4, 11

The Great Race

Introduction to the Learning Center

Introduce Aesop's classic fable of the "Tortoise and the Hare" through this dramatic play center. Students become part of the great race as they hone their listening skills and learn a timeless lesson about perseverance.

Skills & Assessment

- Read a script
- Present a dramatic interpretation
- Assess by staging a play for another class.

Tip

Add an art lesson to this dramatic play by having the students draw sketches of the tortoise and the hare.

Collaborate with a local theater group or drama class to stage the play.

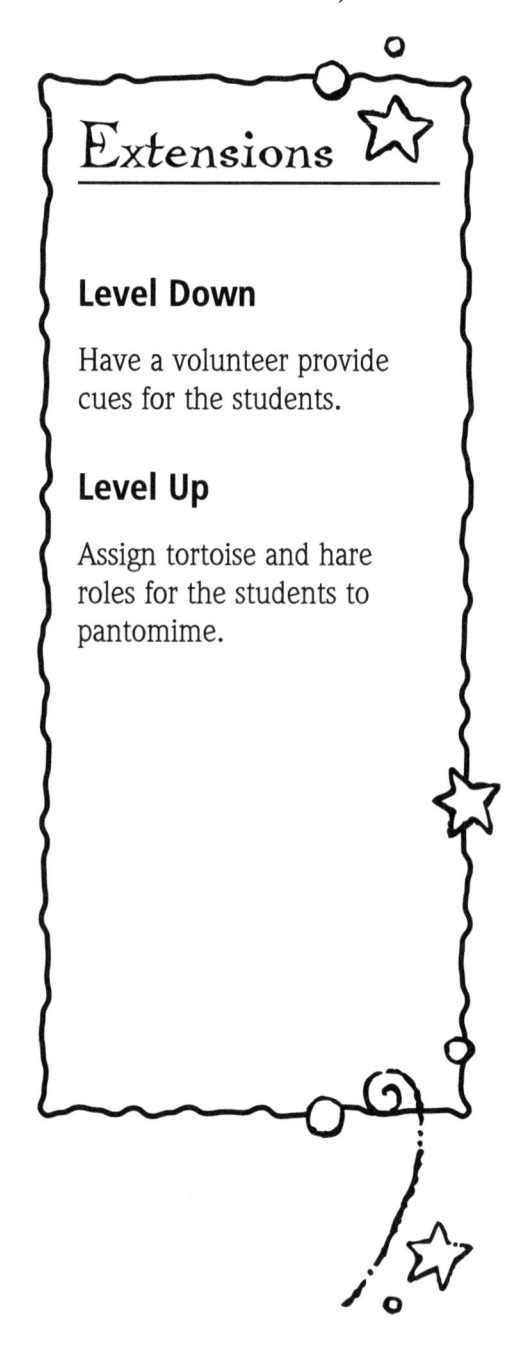

Language Arts   The Great Race, continued

Teacher Materials

- two 11" x 17" sheets of paper
- colored markers
- highlighter marker
- two-panel, self-standing display board
- sign reading "Steady Pace Wins the Race"

Student Materials

- reproducible pages 13 and 14
- one chair for each reader

Teacher Directions

1. Draw or find two simple sketches of the tortoise and the hare. These can be silhouette profiles, heads only, or full bodies.
2. Hang the sketches on the self-standing display board. Hang the "Steady Pace Wins the Race" sign above the sketches.
3. Copy pages 13 and 14 for each student.
4. Decide how many students you want in each performance group. Assign students to the groups.
5. Select the narrator for each group. Have all of the narrators work together with a teacher's aide or volunteer to practice reading their parts.
6. Highlight the student parts to be read in each script.
7. Allow each group time to practice its performance.

Student Directions

1. Work with your group to practice reading the script.
2. Think of ways to show action in your performance.
3. Perform the skit for your class.

Extensions

Level Down

Have a volunteer provide cues for the students.

Level Up

Assign tortoise and hare roles for the students to pantomime.

Name _____ Date _____

The Great Race

A play about the tortoise and the hare.

Narrator: Once upon a time there was a clever rabbit named Mr. Hare. He was very quick on his feet, and when he traveled from place to place, he sounded like this:

Students: Hop-hop-hop.

Narrator: Mr. Hare bragged about how fast he could run. "I can run faster than anyone in the forest," he announced. "I am like a streak of lightning." As he spoke, he swished his hand like a streak of lightning in the sky, like this:

Students: Swish, swish, swish. *(Swish hand like a sword.)*

Narrator: His neighbor, Mr. Tortoise, was tired of Mr. Hare's bragging. "I challenge you to a race," he said. Mr. Hare thought this was so funny that he held his belly and laughed like this:

Students: Ha-ha-ha! Ha-ha-ha! *(Hold hand over belly.)*

Narrator: Everyone in the forest gathered to watch the race. As the race started, Mr. Hare ran down the path like lightning.

Students: Swish, swish, swish. *(Swish hand like a sword.)*

Narrator: Mr. Tortoise was far behind. He moved slowly and made a thumping sound as he walked, like this:

Students: Thump, thump, thump. *(Stomp feet on the floor as you speak.)*

© McGraw-Hill Children's Publishing   0-7682-2941-3 Learning Center Activities for the New Teacher

The Great Race (continued)

Narrator: Mr. Hare was so far ahead in the race that he decided to rest for awhile. He stretched out alongside the path and fell into a deep sleep. He sounded like this:

Students: Snore, wheeeeezzzzz. Snore, wheeeeezzzzz.

Narrator: Mr. Tortoise, on the other hand, kept walking with his steady pace.

Students: Thump, thump, thump. *(Stomp feet on the floor as you speak.)*

Narrator: Mr. Tortoise walked right by Mr. Hare, who slept soundly alongside the road. As Mr. Tortoise neared the finish line, everyone cheered.

Students: Hooray! Hooray! *(Wave arms in the air.)*

Narrator: All the shouting woke up Mr. Hare. He yawned and stretched and began to run again.

Students: Hop-hop-hop.

Narrator: But Mr. Hare was too late. Mr. Tortoise crossed the finish line. He won the race and everyone cheered.

Students: Hooray! Hooray! *(Wave arms in the air.)*

Narrator: Mr. Hare felt very foolish, but by and by he began to feel better. As a reminder of his foolishness, he made a sign to hang over his door. It read:

Students: Steady pace wins the race.

Language Arts

Say It with Feeling

Introduction to the Learning Center

Follow up the dramatic play reading of the "Tortoise and the Hare" with an introduction to punctuation that captures the excitement of the great race. Through this easy-to-prepare center, students will become familiar with sentence expression using a period, a question mark, and an exclamation point.

Skills & Assessment

- Identify and use punctuation for expression
- Assess by having students use each form of punctuation in their own sentences.

Tip

Enrich the enjoyment and understanding of this center by asking students to personify each of the punctuation marks.

Language Arts *Say It with Feeling, continued*

Teacher Materials

- one enlarged copy of *Punctuation Marks* (page 17)
- bulletin board

Student Materials

- reproducible page 18
- pencil

Teacher Directions

1. Copy and cut out the punctuation marks from page 17. If you wish, use a copy machine to enlarge the punctuation marks. Mount them on the bulletin board.
2. Define and discuss each punctuation mark.
3. Hand out the copies of reproducible page 18.
4. Read each sentence aloud with appropriate expression.
5. Complete sentences 1–3 together.
6. Read the remaining sentences aloud again. Cue students as needed to select the appropriate answers.

Student Directions

Follow the directions on your activity page.

Extensions

Level Down

Introduce one type of punctuation at a time. Complete the activity as a group.

Level Up

Have the students complete the activity without additional cues. Ask the students to write their own sentences using each form of punctuation.

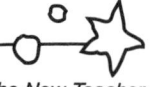

Say It with Feeling, continued

Punctuation Marks

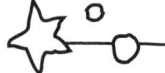

. STOP

!

?

17

Name _____ Date _____

Say It with Feeling!

Listen as each sentence is read.

Decide if the sentence should end with a period (.), a question mark (?), or an exclamation point (!).

1. Mr. Hare bragged about how fast he could run

2. Did Mr. Tortoise brag

3. Go, Mr. Tortoise

4. Mr. Hare and Mr. Tortoise began the race

5. Did Mr. Hare really fall asleep

6. Everyone cheered

7. Mr. Tortoise won

8. Hooray for the winner

Language Arts   *Standards Correlation:*
NCTE 1, 3, 4, 5

May I Take a Message?

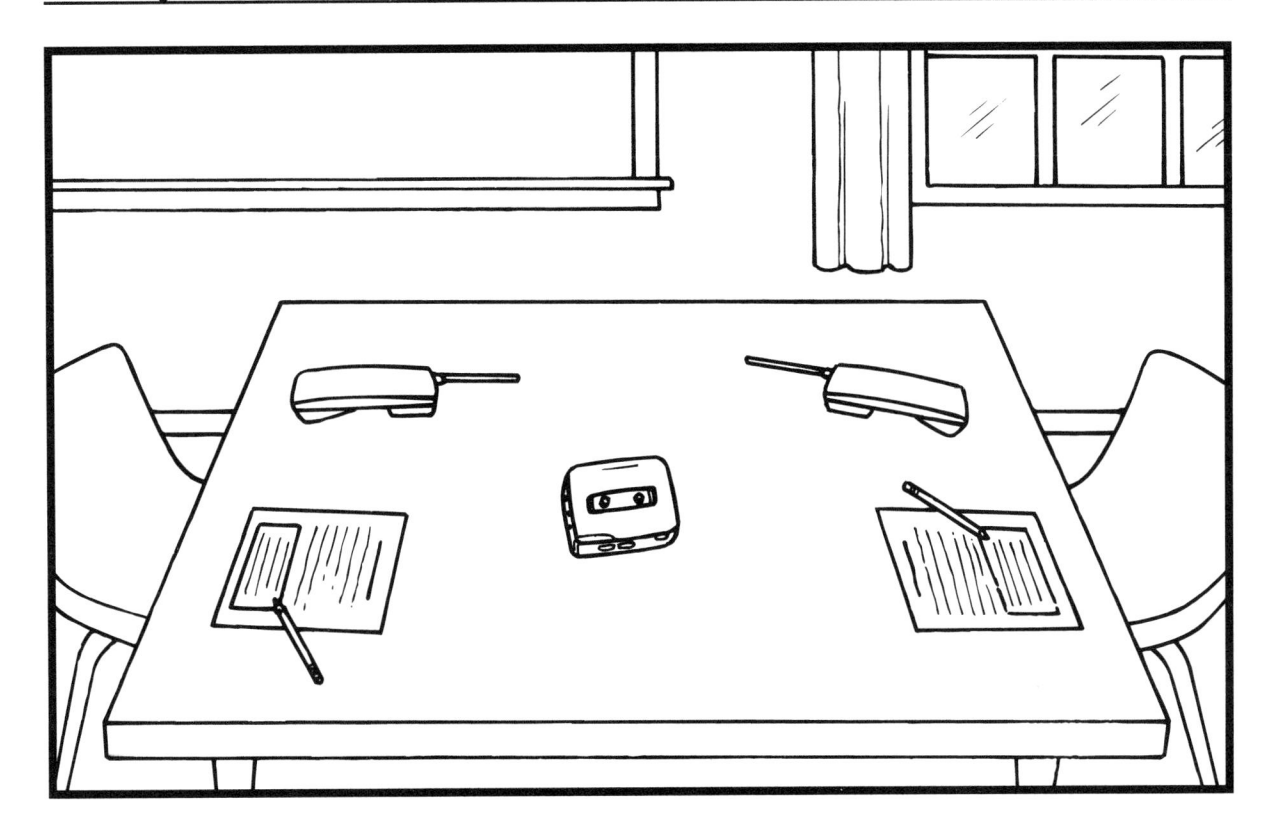

Introduction to the Learning Center

It's never too early to introduce proper telephone skills. The minimal preparation time for this center makes it a lesson that can be repeated throughout the school year. Dramatic play helps reinforce the use of good telephone manners.

Skills & Assessment

- Use telephone etiquette and write down a phone message
- Assess by listening to student-made recordings of their "telephone conversations."

Tip

Contact your local telephone company for programs and activities available to reinforce proper telephone manners and skills.

Help students practice appropriate responses when answering the phone if their parents are not home.

Language Arts *May I Take a Message?, continued*

Teacher Materials

- reproducible page 22
- two telephones
- tape recorder

Student Materials

- reproducible page 21
- pencil

Teacher Directions

1. Set up the center and select teams of two.
2. Discuss and post *Telephone Rules* (page 22). Model several phone conversations before giving each team member *A Message for Mom* (page 21).
3. Read through the activity with the students. Assign roles for message-taker and caller.
4. Tape-record the conversations. Let the students listen to their recordings and decide if they can improve their telephone manners.
5. Have students reverse roles and repeat the activity.

Student Directions

1. Read your part in the telephone call.
2. Write a message to your mom on your activity sheet.

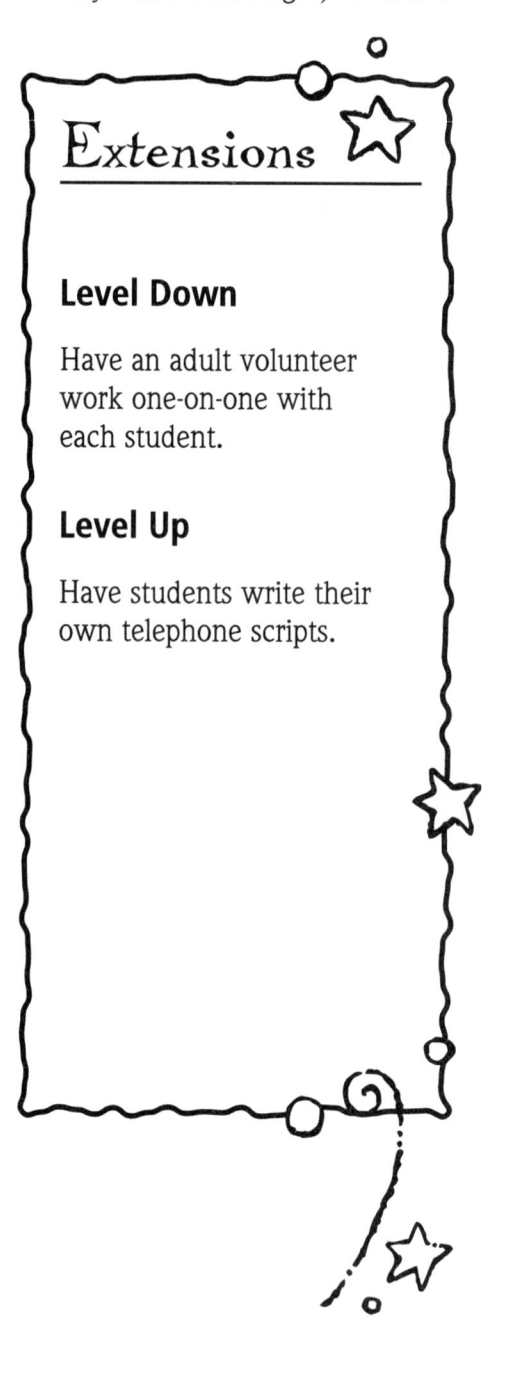

Extensions

Level Down

Have an adult volunteer work one-on-one with each student.

Level Up

Have students write their own telephone scripts.

Name _____ Date _____

A Message for Mom

Message-Taker: Hello.

Caller: Hello, may I speak with your mom?

Message-Taker: Just a moment, please.
(Pause)

Message-Taker: I'm sorry. My mom can't come to the phone right now. Who is calling?

Caller: This is _____.

Message-Taker: I will give her the message that you called.

Caller: Thank you.

Message-Taker: You are welcome. Goodbye.

Telephone Message for Mom

Name of the person who called: _____

Date: _____

Message: _____
_____
_____

Name _____   Date _____

May I Take a Message?

Telephone Rules

1. When you pick up the telephone, say, "Hello."

2. Speak clearly.

3. Do not shout into the telephone receiver.

4. Set the phone down gently.

5. Write down the name of the person who called.

Language Arts

Standards Correlation:
NCTE 4, 5, 9, 12

Field of Friends

Introduction to the Learning Center

Every language has a word for *friend*. Let your students discover new ways of saying the word as they stretch their understanding of other people. This artistic center explores various cultures and makes a statement that can be shared with the whole school.

Skills & Assessment

- Learn the word for *friend* in different languages
- Assess by having students pronounce each new word.

Tip

Enrich this multicultural activity by planning an International Day. Invite volunteers from other countries to share their words for *friend*.

Check with a local lumberyard or craft store to find wooden stakes for the performance display.

Language Arts *Field of Friends, continued*

Teacher Materials

- reproducible pages 25 and 26
- one heavy-duty paper plate
- one yard-long wooden stake
- scissors
- one heavy-duty paper brad
- drill

Student Materials

- reproducible pages 25 and 26
- one heavy-duty paper plate
- one yard-long wooden stake
- scissors
- one heavy-duty paper brad
- colored pencils or markers
- glue

Teacher Directions

1. Copy pages 25 and 26 for each student. Make one extra copy for yourself.
2. Follow the student directions to assemble a sample project.
3. Drill a brad-size hole in each stake.
4. Show the students your sample. Pronounce each word for *friend*. Explain and post the student directions.
5. When all of the students have completed the activity, use a brad to secure each plate to a stake.
6. Hold a "friendship parade" at school. Allow the students to march in the parade with their projects.

Student Directions

1. Color the globe. Cut it out. Glue it to the center of your plate.
2. Write your name on the back of the plate.
3. Color each flag a different color. Cut out the flags.
4. Glue the flags around the globe.
5. Give your plate to your teacher when you are done.

Extensions

Level Down

Assign one word per student and complete as a group activity.

Level Up

Have students research the word for *friend* in different languages. Have them add flags to their displays for each additional language that they learn about.

Field of Friends, continued

Globe Page

friend

Field of Friends, continued

Flag Page

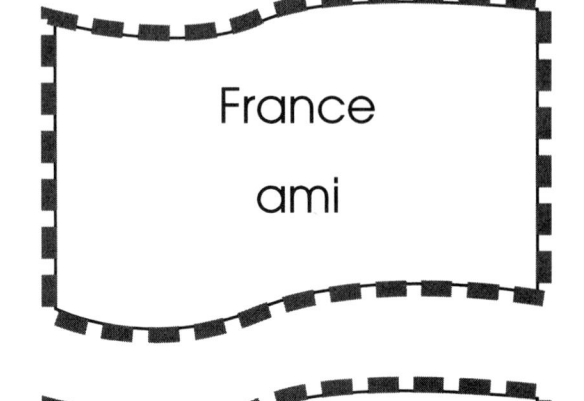

France
ami

Mexico
amigo

Norway
venn

Indonesia
kawan

Kenya
rafiki

Pronunciation Key

ami = ah-me′

amigo = ah-me′-go

kawan = ka-wan′

rafiki = rah-fe′ke

venn = venn

Language Arts *Standards Correlation:*
NCTE 3, 6, 12

Uncle John's Orchard

Introduction to the Learning Center

Every story has a beginning, a middle, and an end. In this center, students will use sequencing skills to order the events in a story about Uncle John's apple orchard.

Skills & Assessment

- Sequence story events
- Create a storyboard
- Assess team presentations of the story.

Tip

Expand this activity into a science-related field trip to a local apple orchard.

Look for educational materials about apples on the Internet.

Language Arts *Uncle John's Orchard, continued*

Teacher Materials

- *Apple Pictures* (page 29) for display
- potted apple tree
- self-standing display board
- pictures of orchards at blossom time and harvesttime
- colored markers
- ribbon
- hole punch

Student Materials

- reproducible pages 29 and 30
- colored pencils or markers
- scissors
- glue

Teacher Directions

1. Color, laminate and cut out one set of *Apple Pictures* (page 29). Punch a hole at the top of each picture. Use ribbon to hang the pictures in the potted apple tree.
2. Decorate the display board with pictures of orchards.
3. Discuss with the students the growing cycle of apples.
4. Explain the directions before giving each student a set of reproducibles.

Student Directions

1. Color the pictures on the *Apple Pictures* sheet.
2. Use the pictures to complete the *Uncle John's Orchard* sheet.

Extensions

Level Down

Cut out the apple pictures in advance for students.

Level Up

Have students write a paragraph about Uncle John's orchard.

Apple Pictures

Color each picture.

Cut out the squares.

The apple is ripe.	The tree blossoms.
The little apple grows.	Uncle John picks the apple.

Name _____   Date _____

Uncle John's Orchard

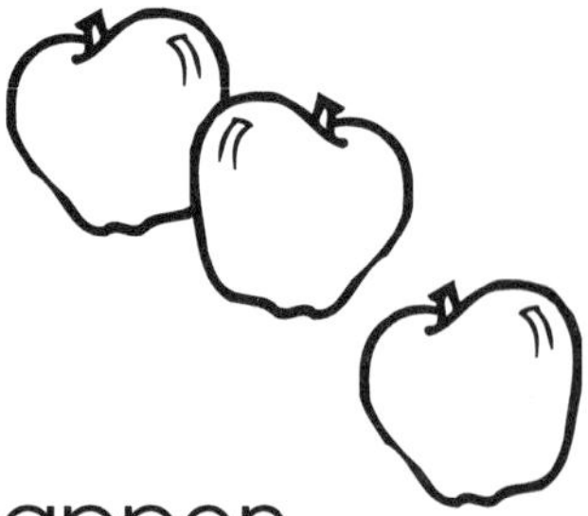

Help Uncle John tell the story of his orchard.
What happens first in the orchard?
Find the picture. Glue it in the first square.
Glue the other pictures in the order that they happen.

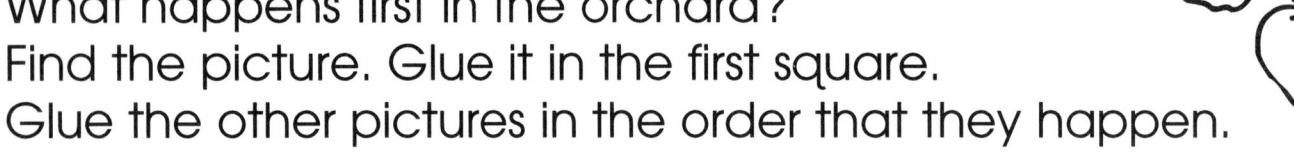

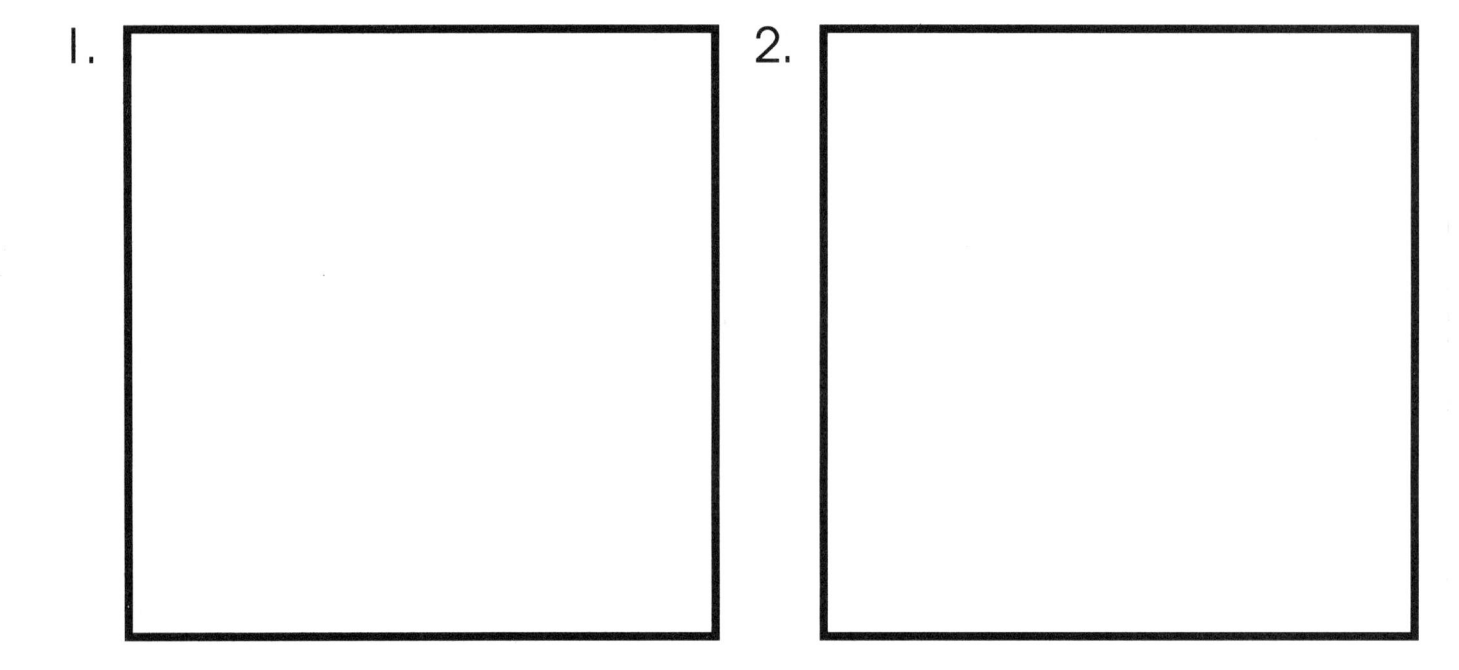

1.

2.

3.

4.

Language Arts *Standards Correlation:*
NCTE 3, 5

The Vowel Game

Introduction to the Learning Center

Learning vowel sounds is easy in this folder-style center for two. Students will improve their skills in spelling as they take turns drawing vowel cards to complete the words on their game boards. There's even a bonus round for an extra challenge. Have some super-speller prizes on hand for the game winners.

Skills & Assessment

- Supply missing vowels to complete words
- Assess through follow-up spelling test.

Tip

Create several of these portable centers as checkout materials for extra practice at home.

Language Arts   *The Vowel Game, continued*

Teacher Materials

- one 12-inch pizza box with lid
- three copies of *Vowel Cards* (page 34)
- one No. 10 envelope
- colored markers
- plain paper to cover pizza box

Student Materials

- *The Vowel Game* (page 33)
- pencil

Teacher Directions

1. Make three copies of *Vowel Cards* (page 34). Color the cards and cut them out. Laminate one set of cards and place them in an envelope labeled "vowel cards."
2. Cover the pizza box with plain paper. Glue the remaining vowel cards to the box. Label the box "The Vowel Game."
3. Place one copy of *The Vowel Game* in the box for each student.
4. Select teams of two for play. Introduce the game and explain the directions to the student.

Student Directions

1. Shuffle the vowel cards and place them facedown in a pile.
2. The first player draws a card.
3. Look at the vowel.
4. Write the vowel in one of the blanks on your activity page to make a word, or pass if you can't make a word.
5. Return the vowel card to the bottom of the deck. Now it's the second player's turn.
6. Repeat steps 2 through 5 until one player has all the blanks filled in. That player is the winner.

Extensions

Level Down

Give students an opportunity to play the game alone to eliminate competition.

Level Up

Have students complete the bonus round.

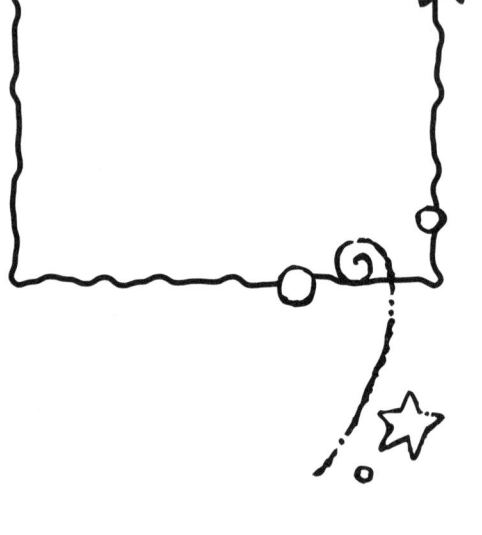

Name _____ Date _____

The Vowel Game

1. h ___ t
2. f ___ x
3. m ___ d
4. wh ___ t
5. s ___ w
6. l ___ g
7. ___ sk
8. n ___ w
9. b ___ s
10. s ___ n

Bonus Round:

11. cl ___ p
12. j ___ k ___
13. sm ___ l ___
14. r ___ ___ n
15. fr ___ g
16. pl ___ n ___ t
17. n ___ n ___
18. b ___ rn
19. d ___ rt
20. ___ sl ___ nd

33

© McGraw-Hill Children's Publishing   0-7682-2941-3 Learning Center Activities for the New Teacher

Language Arts — *The Vowel Game, continued*

Vowel Cards

a	e
i	o
u	

34

Math

Standards Correlation:
NCTM Numbers and Operations 1 NCTM Measurement 1

The Celebration Calendar

Introduction to the Learning Center

Mathematics and poetry are blended together in this center. A popular calendar poem will help students learn how many days are in each month and will guide students in creating calendars for their birth months. Collect all of the calendars for a special year-long display of student birthdays.

Skills & Assessment

- Learn the number of days in each month
- Create a birth-month calendar
- Assess through group recitation and presentation.

Tip

Have students memorize the poem so they'll always know how many days are in each month.

Math *The Celebration Calendar, continued*

Teacher Materials

- 12 copies of *Celebration Calendar* (page 37)
- four copies of *Calendar Poem* (page 38)
- one square box
- a birthday balloon bouquet
- colored markers
- one self-adhesive gold star for each student

Student Materials

- reproducible pages 37 and 38
- pencil
- colored pencils or markers

Teacher Directions

1. Make 12 copies of *Celebration Calendar* (page 37) to create a full-year calendar sample.
2. Make four copies of *Calendar Poem* (page 38). Color them and glue one to each side of a square box. Use the box to anchor the balloon bouquet.
3. Prepare a list of the students' birthdays.
4. Introduce the center and recite the poem, using the sample calendar as a model.
5. Give each student a *Celebration Calendar* to create a calendar for the month of his or her birth. Let the students use your sample calendar as a guide.
6. When all of the students have completed the activity, collect the calendars and display them in the classroom. Have your students recite the poem for another class.

Student Directions

1. Look at the sample calendar.
2. Use your calendar page to make a calendar for the month of your birth.
3. Say the poem as you work.
4. Color your calendar page.
5. Stick a big star on your birthday.

Extensions

Level Down

Number the calendar pages in advance.

Level Up

Have students work in groups to prepare full-year calendars.

Name _____   Date _____

Celebration Calendar

SATURDAY					
FRIDAY					
THURSDAY					
WEDNESDAY					
TUESDAY					
MONDAY					
SUNDAY					

The Celebration Calendar, continued

The Calendar Poem

Thirty days hath September

April, June, and November.

All the rest have thirty-one,

Except for February which stands alone

At twenty-eight most of the time

Excepting leap year. That's twenty-nine!

Math

Standards Correlation:
NCTM Geometry 1, 2, 4

Geometry George and Jane

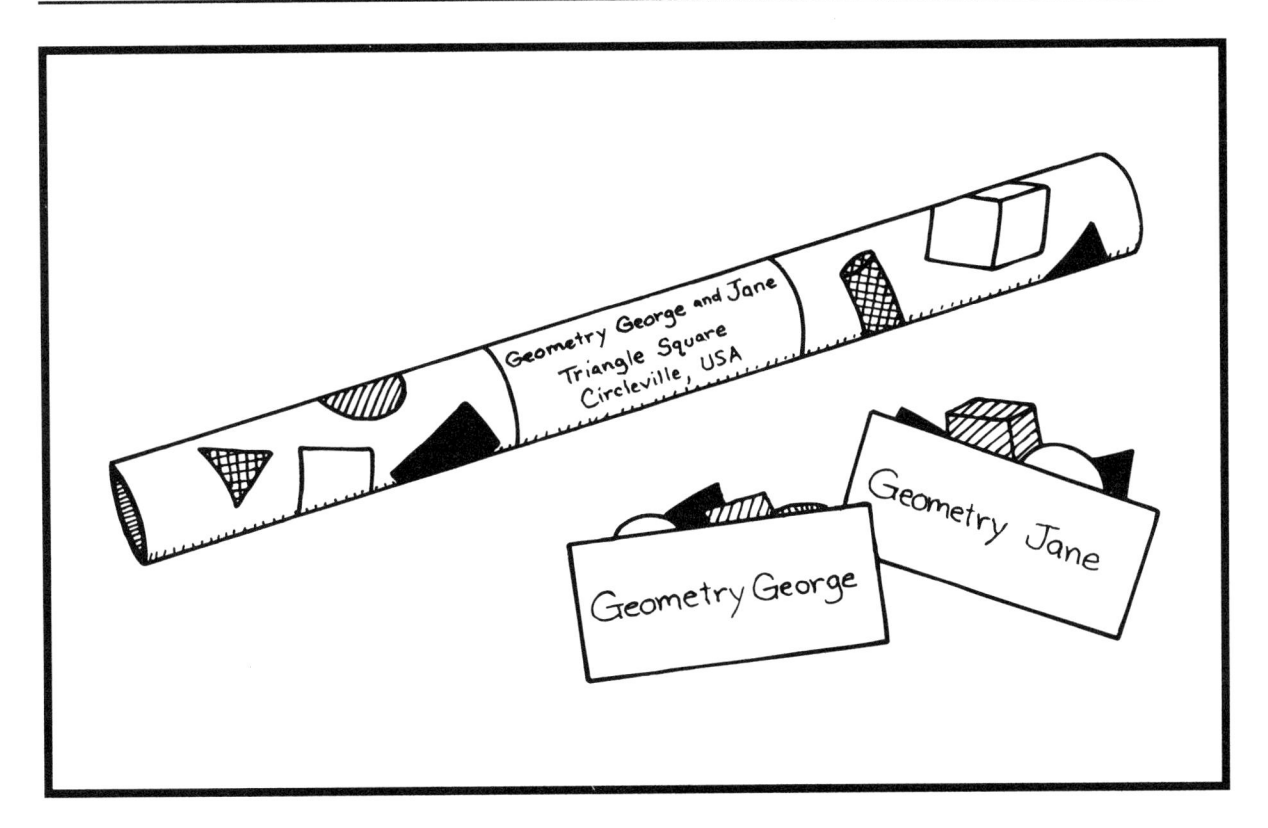

Introduction to the Learning Center

Help students learn the names of shapes with Geometry George and Geometry Jane. This folder-style center is great for imaginative students, as well as reluctant learners who need to reinforce their knowledge of flat and solid geometric shapes.

Skills & Assessment

- Identify and use geometric shapes to design figures
- Assess by having each student describe his or her designs.

Tip

Turn this center into a language arts activity by having students tell a story about each of their designs.

Expand the center even further by displaying art reproductions that are based on geometric forms. Students will enjoy Alexander Calder's fanciful mobiles.

Math   Geometry George and Jane, *continued*

Teacher Materials

- four copies each of reproducible pages 41 and 42
- colored construction paper
- colored markers
- one 24-inch mailing tube
- two No. 10 envelopes
- address label reading:

    Geometry George and Geometry Jane
    Triangle Square
    Circleville, USA

Student Materials

- one sheet of construction paper
- pencil

Teacher Directions

1. Make four copies of *Geometry George* (page 41) on one color of construction paper. Make four copies of *Geometry Jane* (page 42) on a different color of construction paper.

2. Cut out all of the shapes. Laminate one set of the *Geometry George* shapes and one set of the *Geometry Jane* shapes.

3. Label one envelope "Geometry George" and one envelope "Geometry Jane." Put the laminated shapes in their corresponding envelopes. Place the envelopes inside the mailing tube.

4. Glue the remaining shapes on the outside of the mailing tube. Glue the address label to the tube.

5. Introduce the center. Identify each of the shapes and explain the directions.

Student Directions

1. Take Geometry George's shapes out of his envelope.

2. Arrange them on your desk until George has a head, a body, arms, and legs.

3. When you have a design you like, trace the shapes onto a sheet of construction paper. Color your design.

4. Repeat using the other envelope with Geometry Jane's shapes. Trace your design onto the backside of your construction paper. Color your design.

5. Tell your teacher or a partner about the shapes you used.

Extensions

Level Down

Use only the Geometry George shapes.

Level Up

Make several laminated sets of shapes for students to create a series of geometric figures.

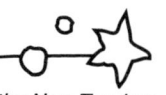

Geometry George and Jane, continued

Geometry George

41

Geometry George and Jane, continued

Geometry Jane

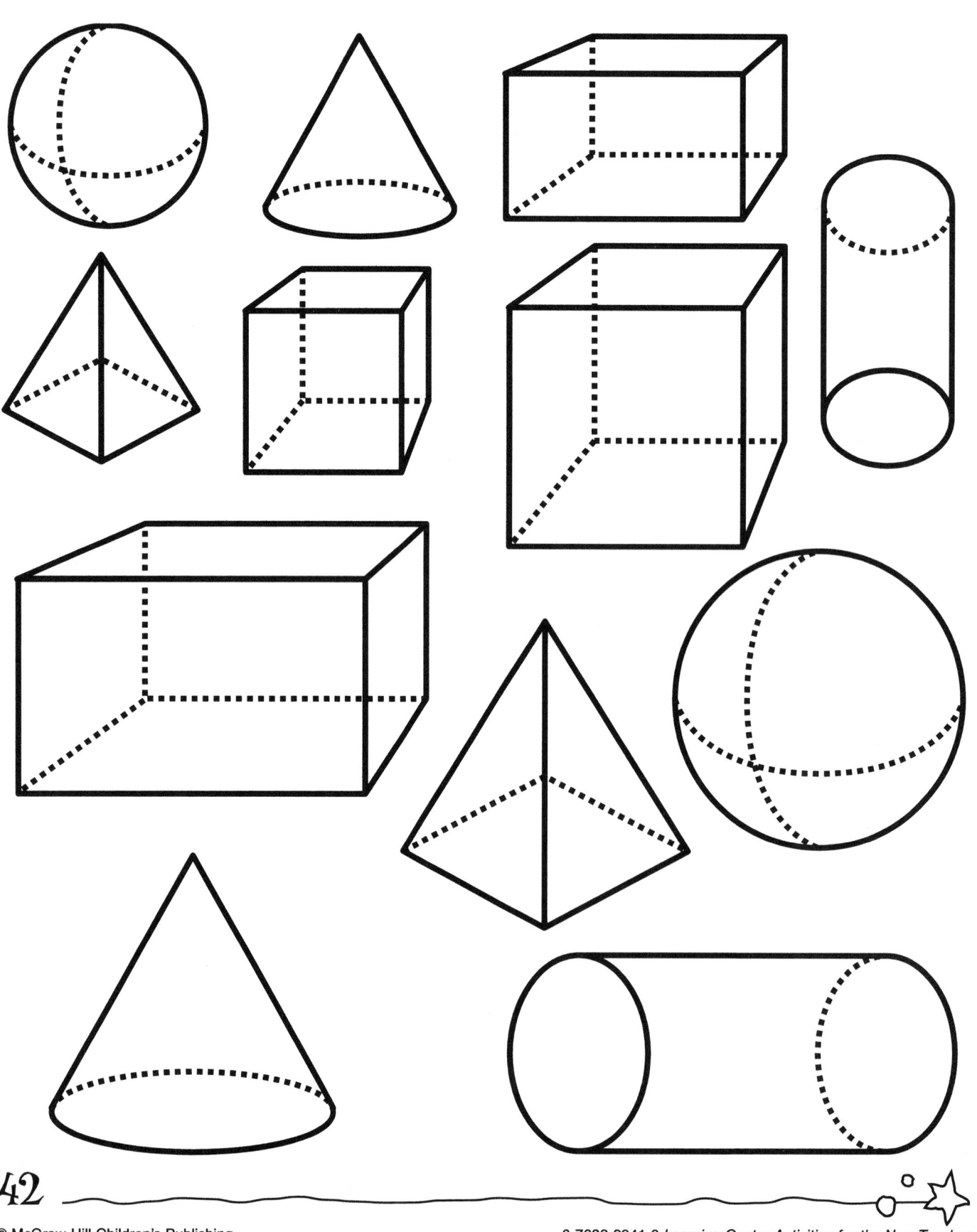

Math

Standards Correlation:
NCTM Algebra 1, 4

Colorful Cottage

Introduction to the Learning Center

Yikes! The three little pigs can't decide on a pattern for their new cottage roof, so they are asking students for help. Challenge the students to use various styles of roof tiles to create a multi-colored roof just right for a fairy-tale life in the forest.

Skills & Assessment

- Create a pattern
- Assess by having students explain the patterns they created.

Tip

Use this center as a follow-up activity after reading the classic fairy tale.

Math Colorful Cottage, *continued*

Teacher Materials

- reproducible pages 45 and 46
- flannel board
- pieces of felt
- markers
- glue
- hook-and-loop fastener stick-ons
- shoe box

Student Materials

- reproducible pages 45 and 46
- glue
- colored pencils, crayons, or markers

Teacher Directions

1. Copy pages 45 and 46 for each student. Make one extra copy of each page.

2. Color one copy of page 45 and one copy of page 46. Cut out the pieces and laminate them. Stick one half of the hook-and-loop fasteners on each section of the cottage roof. Glue a piece of felt to the back of the cottage. Place the cottage on the flannel board. Stick the other half of the hook-and-loop fasteners to the back of each roof tile piece.

3. Place the prepared roof tiles in a shoe box.

4. Introduce the center and explain the directions.

Student Directions

1. Help the three little pigs choose a pattern for their cottage roof. Use the flannel board pieces to practice creating a pattern on the roof.

2. When you have a pattern you like, color the roof tiles on your activity page.

3. Cut out the roof tiles and glue them to the roof on your cottage page.

Extensions

Level Down

Have students work in groups to create the pattern for the cottage roof.

Level Up

Have students color unique designs on the cottage roof pattern.

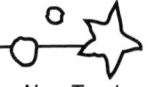

Roof Tiles

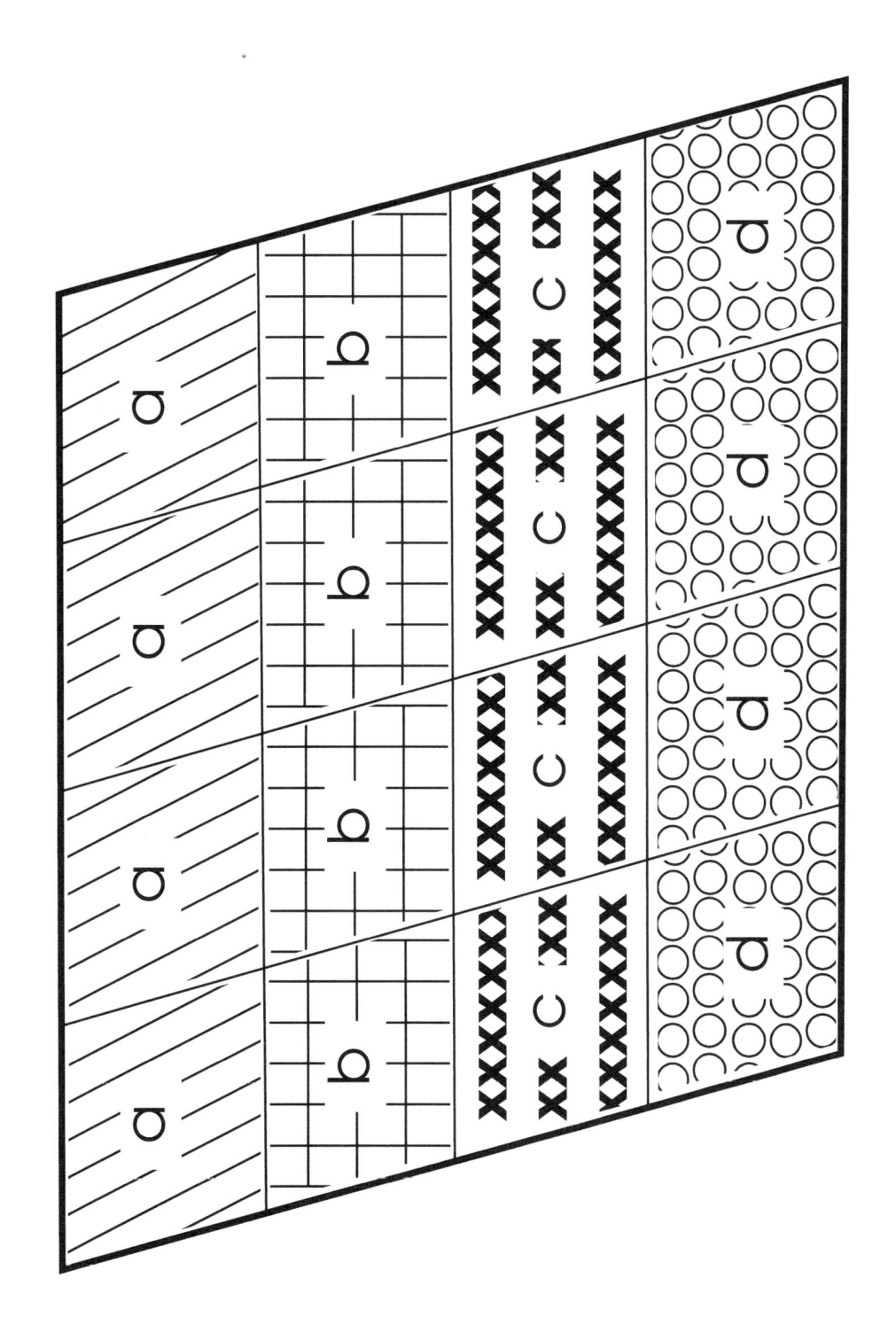

45

Name _____ Date _____

The Three Little Pigs' Cottage

46

Math

Standards Correlation:
NCTM Geometry 2

Grandpa Elmer's Cupboard

Introduction to the Learning Center

Help students understand the concepts of relative position and the terms of *left, right, top, middle,* and *bottom.* Students will practice locating different flavors of jelly in "Grandpa Elmer's Jelly Cupboard."

Skills & Assessment

- Understand and use vocabulary words to describe the locations of objects
- Assess by rearranging the jars and having the students put them back in order.

Tip

This center can become a multi-discipline adventure. Add samples or photographs of each of the fruits for a science lesson. Have students design original labels for the different jellies in an art center. And for a yummy treat, set up a taste-test challenge for each flavor.

Math *Grandpa Elmer's Cupboard, continued*

Teacher Materials

- three-shelf bookcase
- nine 8-ounce jars
- *Labels* (page 49)
- colored markers
- glue
- one large sign reading "Grandpa Elmer's Jelly Cupboard"

Student Materials

- reproducible page 50
- pencil

Teacher Directions

1. Make a copy of *Labels* (page 49). Color and cut out the labels. Glue them onto the jars. Prepare the cupboard sign.
2. Set up the center. *Be sure to put the jars in the order in which they appear on the label page.*
3. Introduce and explain the center. Read each of the jelly labels with students and discuss the vocabulary words.
4. Give each student a copy of *Grandpa Elmer's Jelly Cupboard* (page 50). Allow them to use the jelly cupboard station to find each answer.

Student Directions

1. Read the statements on your paper.
2. Look at the jelly jars in the cupboard to find the answers.
3. Circle the correct answers on your page.

Extensions

Level Down

Read the sentences aloud to the students.

Level Up

Cover up the answer choices on the worksheet. Have the students write descriptions for the locations of each jelly jar.

Grandpa Elmer's Cupboard, continued

Labels

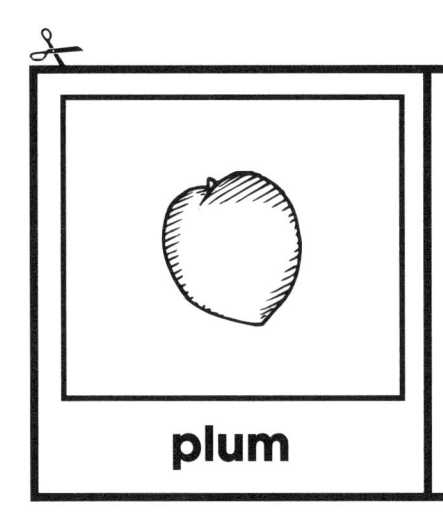

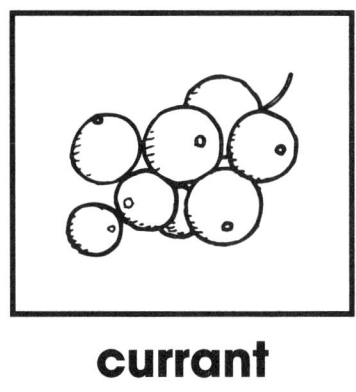

plum	**currant**	**strawberry**
top shelf left	top shelf middle	top shelf right
grape	**prickly pear**	**apple**
middle shelf left	middle shelf middle	middle shelf right
blackberry	**raspberry**	**peach**
bottom shelf left	bottom shelf middle	bottom shelf right

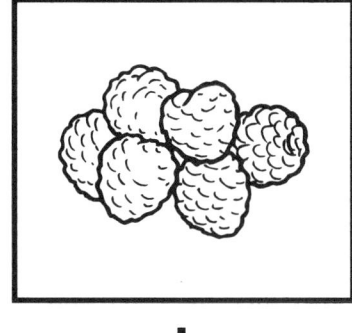

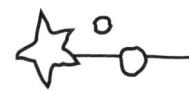

Name _____ Date _____

Grandpa Elmer's Jelly Cupboard

Help Grandpa Elmer find his favorite jelly for each day of the week.

1. **Monday**
   The jelly on the top shelf on the right side is _____.
   a. strawberry   b. peach

2. **Tuesday**
   The grape jelly is on the _____.
   a. bottom shelf   b. middle shelf

3. **Wednesday**
   The currant jelly is on the _____.
   a. top shelf in the middle
   b. bottom shelf on the left

4. **Thursday**
   The jelly on the bottom shelf on the left is _____.
   a. blackberry   b. prickly pear

5. It's **Friday**! Pick your favorite jelly.
   Write the name here:

   _____

   Describe its location here:

   _____

Critter Contest

Introduction to the Learning Center

Making a graph is more fun than a barrel of monkeys in this easy-to-use center. After students cast votes for their favorite animals, teams sort, count, and record the results on a graph. Which animal will be in the winner's circle? It's the students' choice. Ask a volunteer to sit in as a voting supervisor.

Skills & Assessment

- Sort and count ballots
- Record voting results in a graph
- Assess by having students present their graphs.

Tip

Tie this center in with a lesson on democracy and the importance of voting.

Teacher Materials

- *Critter Candidates* (page 54)
- flannel board
- felt
- colored markers
- one "Critter Contest" sign
- ballot box

Math Critter Contest, continued

Student Materials

- reproducible pages 53 and 54
- pencil

Teacher Directions

1. Make a "Critter Contest" sign. Post it on the flannel board.
2. Make one copy of *Critter Candidates* (page 54). Color, cut out, and laminate the pictures. Glue a felt square on the back of each picture and place the picture on the flannel board.
3. To make the ballots, copy enough of the *Critter Candidates* page for your students. Cut the pages apart as indicated. Separate the pictures and place them in three stacks next to the ballot box.
4. Instruct the students on how to select a ballot, fold it in half, and place it in the ballot box.
5. After the entire class has voted, select teams of three.
6. Explain the directions for counting the ballots and recording the results on a graph. Give each student a copy of *Critter Contest Results* (page 53).
7. After all the teams have completed their graphs, have the students stage a mock press conference to announce the results.

Student Directions

1. Take out one ballot from the box.
2. Look at the ballot. Is it a monkey, a whale, or a tiger?
3. Put all the monkeys in one stack, all the whales in another stack, and all the tigers in a third stack.
4. After all the ballots are out of the box, count the monkey ballots.
5. Color a box by the monkey on your graph for each monkey vote.
6. Repeat for the whale ballots and the tiger ballots.
7. Count the number of colored boxes for each animal. Fill in the blanks at the bottom of the page.

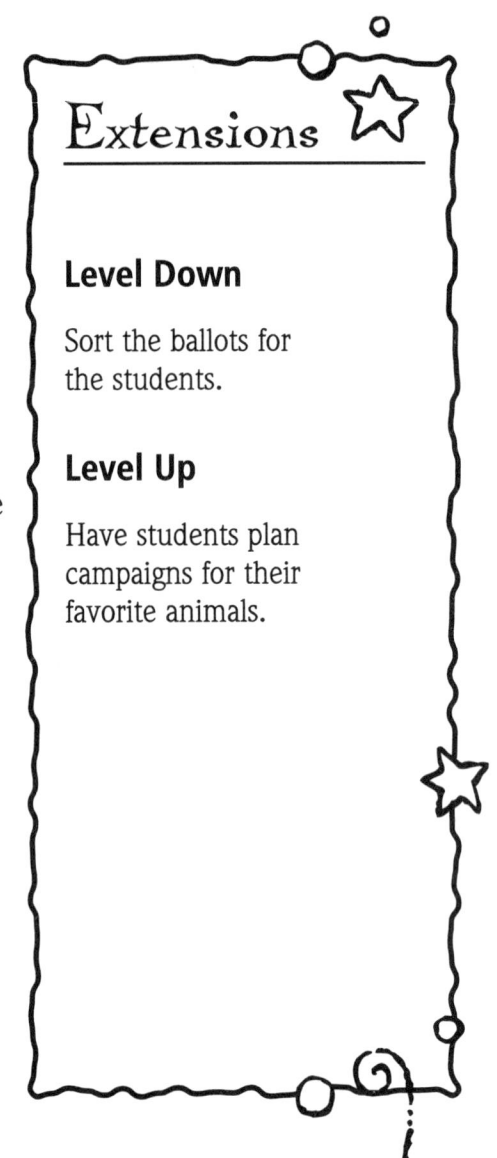

Extensions

Level Down

Sort the ballots for the students.

Level Up

Have students plan campaigns for their favorite animals.

© McGraw-Hill Children's Publishing 0-7682-2941-3 Learning Center Activities for the New Teacher

Name _____ Date _____

Critter Contest Results

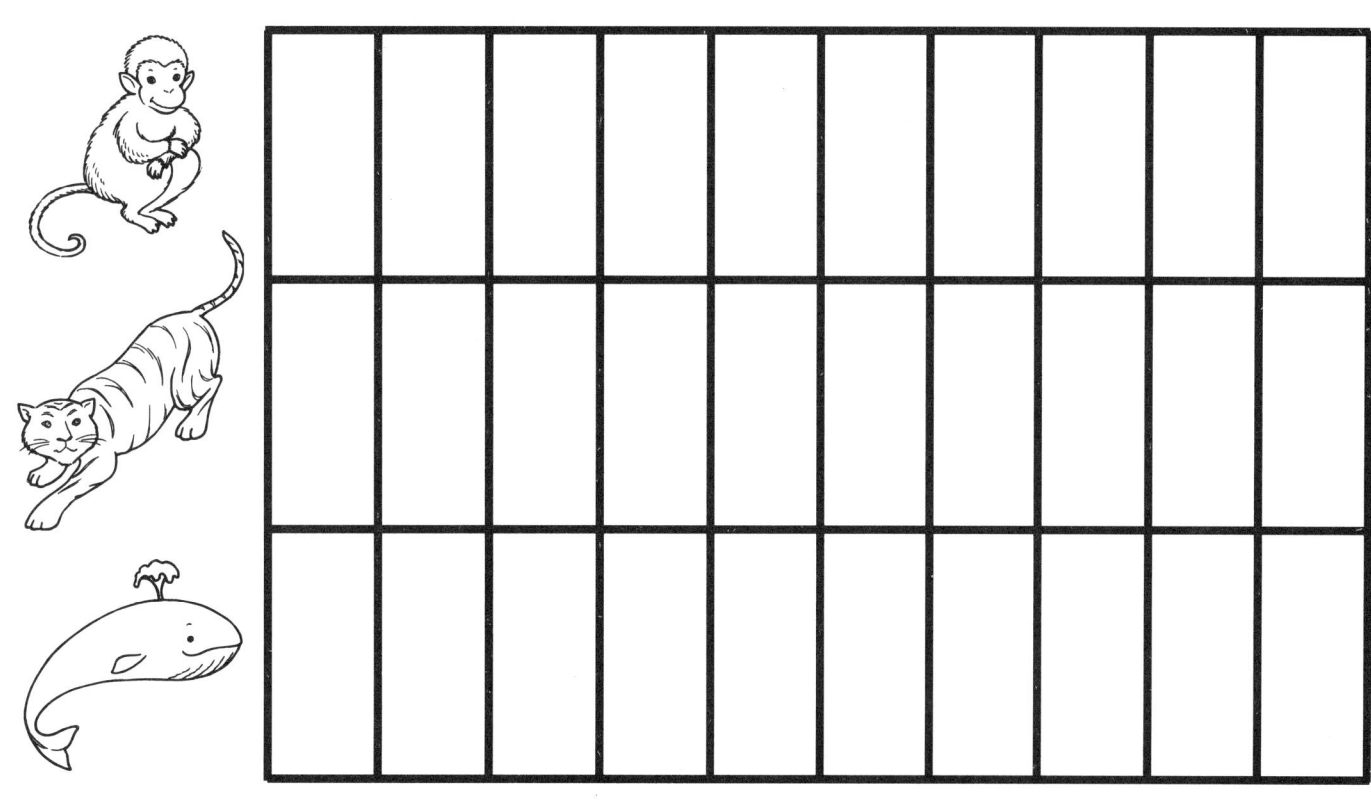

Contest Results

1. The 🐒 had _____ votes.

2. The 🐅 had _____ votes.

3. The 🐋 had _____ votes.

4. The winner is the _____.

Critter Contest, continued

Critter Candidates

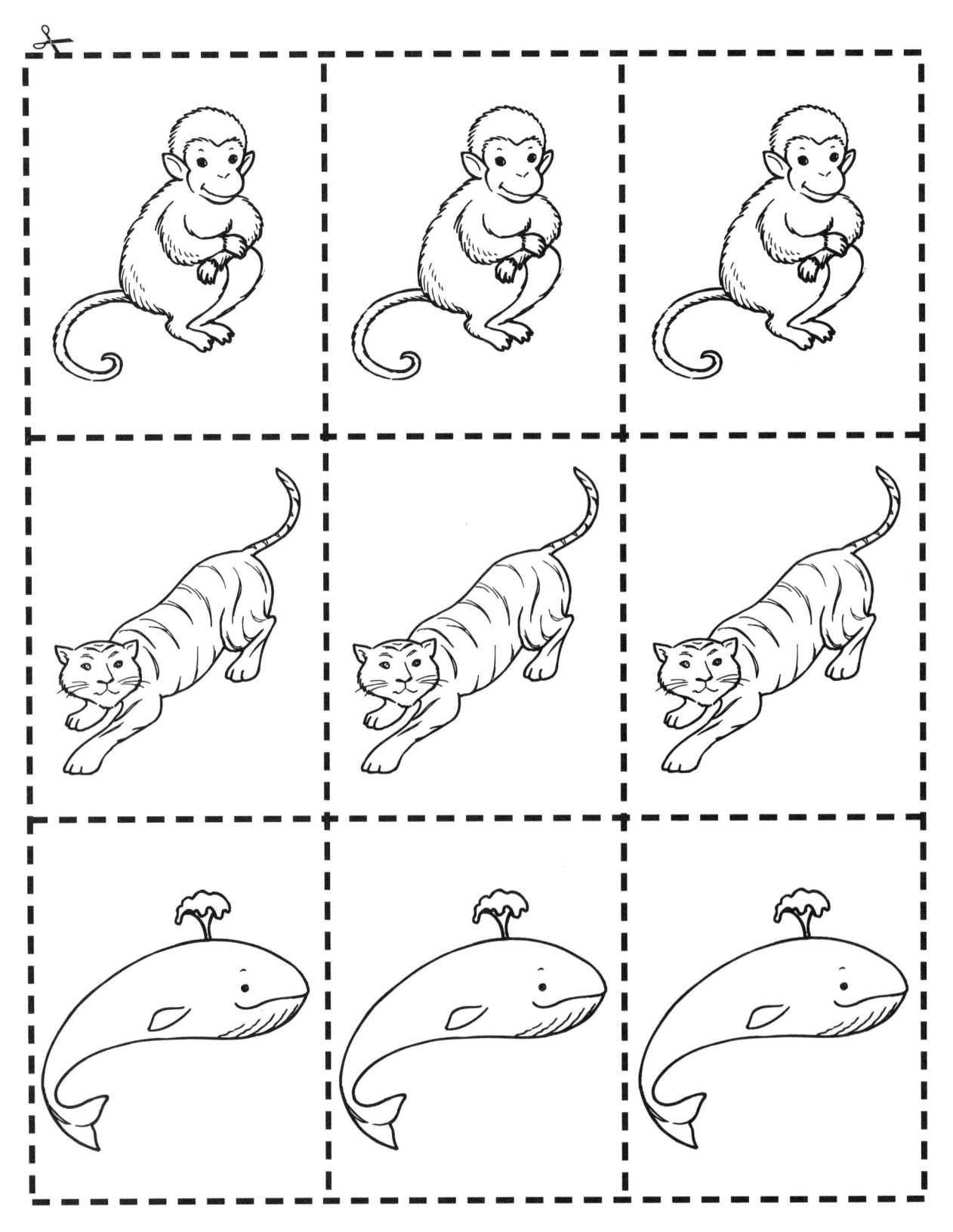

54

© McGraw-Hill Children's Publishing

0-7682-2941-3 *Learning Center Activities for the New Teacher*

Math

Shopping at the General Store

Introduction to the Learning Center

This center reinforces skills in counting money. Students will enjoy the dramatic-play activities in this simple general store, as they take turns acting as a shopper and a store clerk.

Skills & Assessment

- Understand and use currencies of penny, nickel, dime, quarter, and half-dollar
- Assess by having students report how much was spent.

Tip

Turn this into a folder-style desk activity for two. Laminate the activity pages and place them in the "General Store" shoe box, along with a coin purse for shopping.

Teacher Materials

- shoe box
- one *General Store* reproducible (page 57)
- two *Coins* reproducibles (page 58)
- items for the "General Store":
  banana, mini chocolate bar, small rubber ball, pack of stickers, erasers
- coin purse
- apron

Student Materials

- reproducible page 57

Math *Shopping at the General Store, continued*

Teacher Directions

1. Set up an old-fashioned store. Stock the store with the items shown on *General Store* (page 57).

2. Copy, cut out, and laminate two pages of *Coins* (page 58). Put one set of coins in the coin purse and one set in the shoe box.

3. Copy *General Store* (page 57) for each student. Put an extra copy in the store.

4. Introduce the center. Explain and post the student directions.

5. Select teams of two for the center. Have one student wear the apron and act as the clerk. Have the other student carry the coin purse and act as the shopper.

Student Directions

Shopper

1. Look at your copy of *General Store*. This is your shopping list.

2. Decide what you would like to buy.

3. Circle the items on your list.

4. Hand your list to the clerk. Wait for the clerk to collect your items and total your bill.

5. Pay the clerk for the items.

Clerk

1. Look at the items the shopper wants to buy.

2. Collect the items.

3. Tell the shopper how much to pay.

4. Count the money. Give the shopper any change he or she should get.

Shopper and Clerk

Take turns being the shopper and the clerk. After each turn, return the items to the store and the coins to the coin purse or cash box.

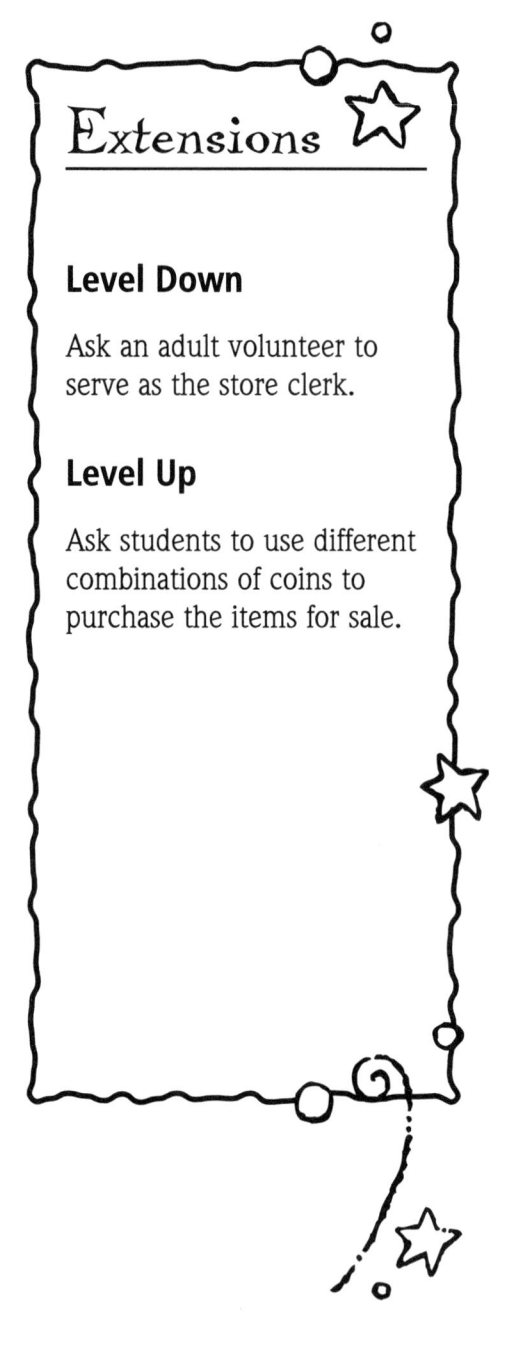

Extensions

Level Down

Ask an adult volunteer to serve as the store clerk.

Level Up

Ask students to use different combinations of coins to purchase the items for sale.

Shopping at the General Store, continued

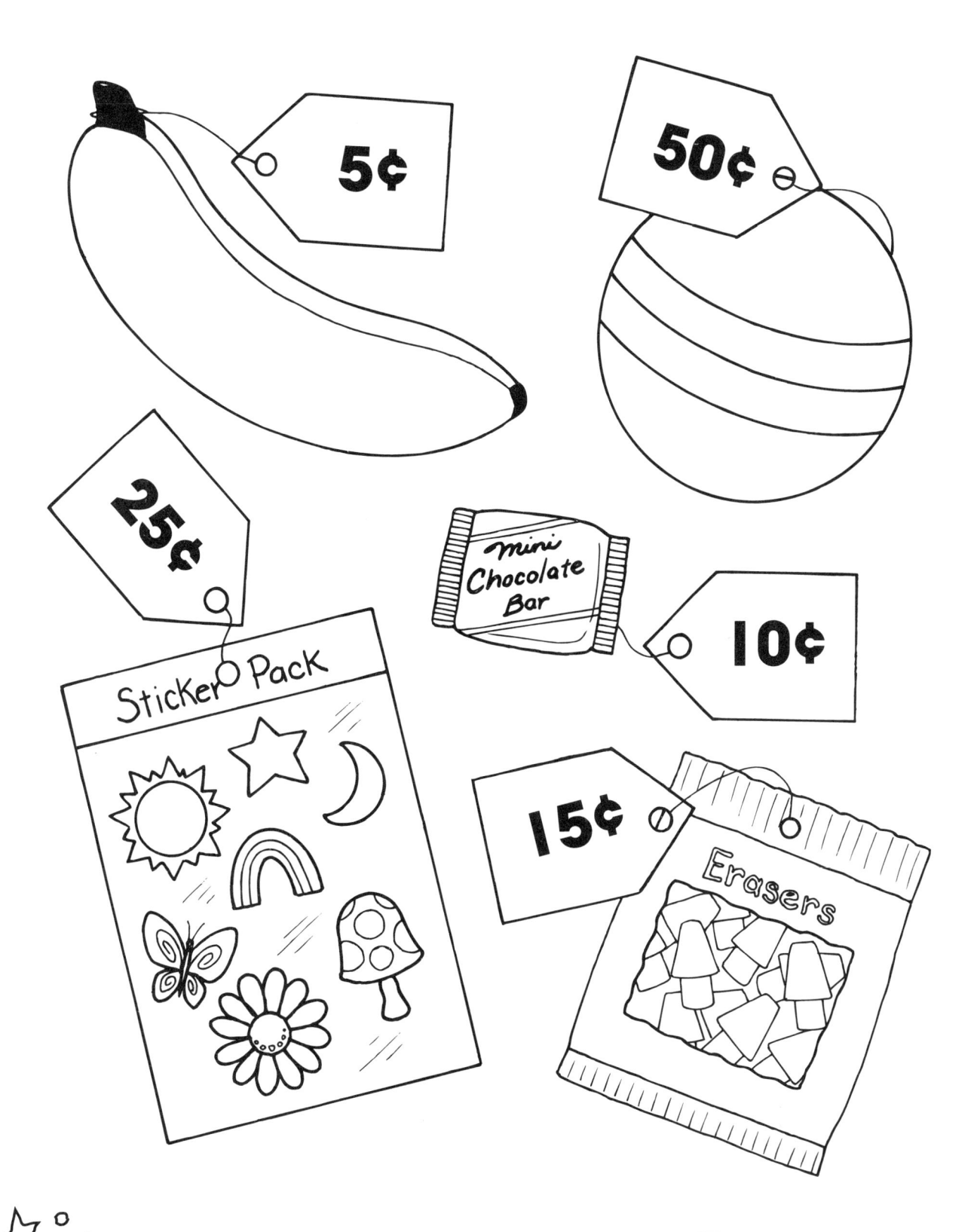

General Store

- 5¢ (banana)
- 50¢ (ball)
- 25¢ (Sticker Pack)
- 10¢ (mini Chocolate Bar)
- 15¢ (Erasers)

57

© McGraw-Hill Children's Publishing 0-7682-2941-3 *Learning Center Activities for the New Teacher*

Shopping at the General Store, continued

Coins

Math

Standards Correlation:
NCTM Number and Operations 1, 2

Squirrel Sort

Introduction to the Learning Center

All the squirrels got mixed up and only the students can help! This sorting center is perfect for autumn, when squirrels are readying for the winter. A harvest filled with a variety of nuts will give students a hands-on sorting adventure. This activity ties in perfectly with your seasonal projects.

Skills & Assessment

- Sort and classify objects
- Assess by holding a sorting marathon for the whole class.

Tip

Tie this instant center in with other autumn displays in the classroom or create a display with bushel baskets and produce that can be used for hands-on sorting as a culminating activity.

Be sure that you are aware of any student allergies before implementing this center. Any students who are allergic to nuts must be given alternative objects to sort.

Math *Squirrel Sort, continued*

Teacher Materials

- one large bowl
- a collection of mixed nuts, in shells
- *Bushel Baskets* (page 62)
- one 8-ounce plastic cup for each type of nut
- glue

Student Materials

- *Mixed Nuts* (page 61)
- crayons

Teacher Directions

1. Make enough copies of *Bushel Baskets* (page 62) so that you have one basket for each type of nut. Cut out the baskets. Write the names of the nuts on the baskets and glue a sample nut to each basket. Glue one basket to each plastic cup.
2. Pour the mixed nuts into the bowl.
3. Copy page 61. Write the names of the nuts on the graph. Then make a copy for each student.
4. Set up and introduce the center.

Student Directions

1. Take one nut from the bowl.
2. What kind of nut is it?
3. Place it in the correct bushel basket.
4. When you have sorted all of the nuts, count how many of each kind you have.
5. Color one box on the graph for every five nuts.

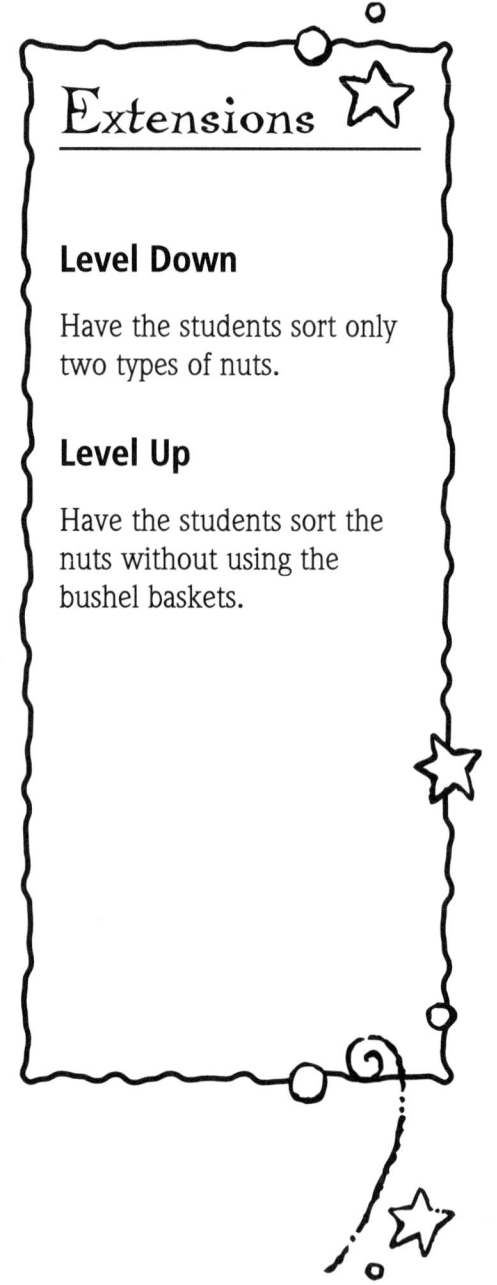

Extensions

Level Down

Have the students sort only two types of nuts.

Level Up

Have the students sort the nuts without using the bushel baskets.

Mixed Nuts

40
35
30
25
20
15
10
5

Bushel Baskets

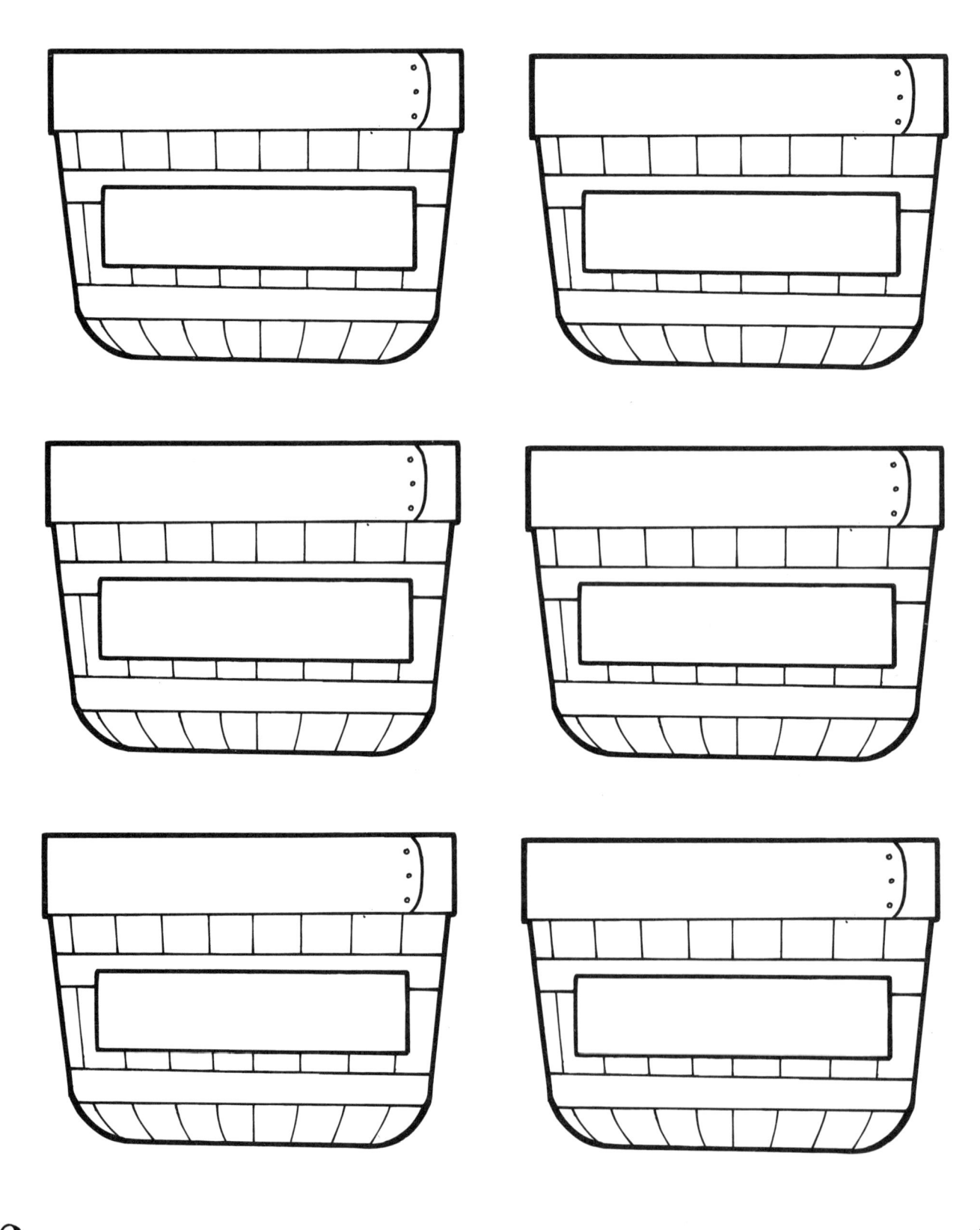

Squirrel Sort, continued

Math

How Many Tomatoes?

Introduction to the Learning Center

In this counting center, students will use manipulatives to solve story problems. They will demonstrate their knowledge of addition and subtraction as they build paper tomato plants.

Skills & Assessment

- Use addition and subtraction to solve story problems
- Assess by having students compare their "tomato plants" to the model you create.

Tip

Add a science lesson to this center by allowing students to grow tomato plants right in the classroom. Have the students record their observations of the plants' development and collect tomato-based recipes to prepare after the harvest.

Math *How Many Tomatoes?, continued*

Teacher Materials

- red construction paper
- tomato plant or tree branch with limbs
- paper clips
- scissors
- one small paper plate for each student
- cloth

Student Materials

- reproducible pages 65 and 66
- pencil
- glue
- colored pencils or markers

Teacher Directions

1. For each student, cut out twelve 1-inch circles from red construction paper. Place each set of circles on a paper plate.
2. Cut out another twelve circles for the tomato plant display. Attach four circles to the plant with paper clips. Set the other circles aside.
3. Cover the plant with a cloth.
4. Copy pages 65 and 66 for each student.
5. When everyone has completed the activity, uncover the tomato plant so that each student can determine if his or her tomato plant matches yours.

Student Directions

1. Read the story problems on *How Many Tomatoes?* (page 65).
2. Place the red circles on the *Henry's Tomato Plant* page to show the answer to each problem.
3. How many tomatoes did Henry's plant have at the end? Glue that many red circles to your tomato plant picture.

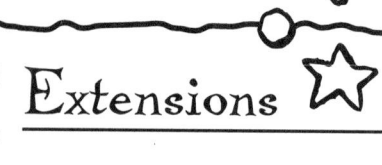

Extensions

Level Down

Let the students work in groups to paper clip circles to the tomato plant model.

Level Up

Create more story questions for students to solve.

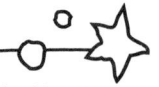

Name _____ Date _____

How Many Tomatoes?

Henry planted a tomato plant. He watched his tomatoes grow.

Read the stories.

Use your paper tomatoes to help you solve the problems.

1. One morning, Henry counted two tomatoes. Place two tomatoes on your tomato plant. _____	4. Rascal the raccoon ate three tomatoes. How many tomatoes are left on the plant now? _____
2. The next day, Henry counted five more tomatoes. How many tomatoes are on the plant now? _____	5. Henry was hungry. He ate two tomatoes. How many tomatoes are left on the plant now? _____
3. Henry counted three more tomatoes. How many tomatoes are on the plant now? _____	6. Henry gave one tomato to Luz. How many tomatoes are left on the plant now? _____

Name _____ Date _____

Henry's Tomato Plant

Science

Insect Inventory

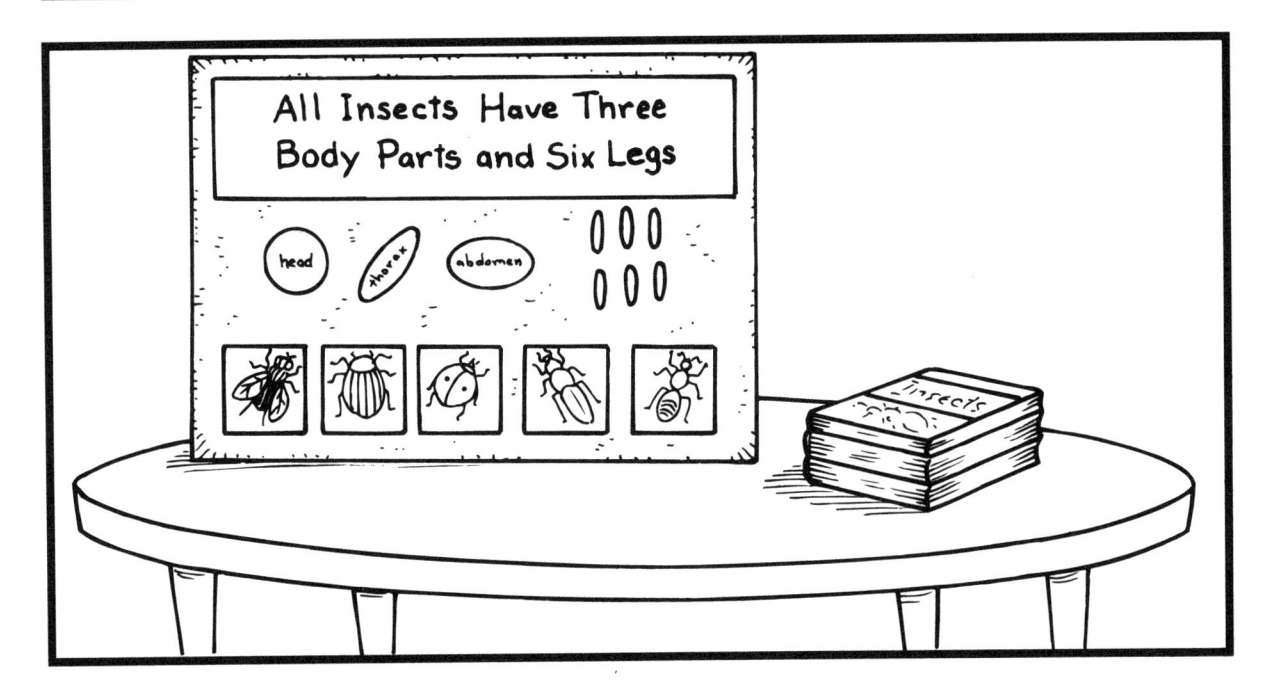

Introduction to the Learning Center

Insects are everywhere, from the tropics to the polar regions. Introduce students to the common characteristics of this animal class. This discovery center taps into the imagination to let students create and name their own insects.

Skills & Assessment

- Identify common insect characteristics
- Assess by having students design imaginary insects to demonstrate the characteristics.

Tip

Borrow an insect display from a local university or library. Allow students to study the display and identify some of the insects featured.

Science   Insect Inventory, continued

Teacher Materials

- *Insect Parts* (page 69)
- insect pictures and books
- scissors
- small felt squares
- glue
- strip of construction paper
- marker
- flannel board

Student Materials

- a variety of felt scraps
- scissors
- *Insect Inventory* (page 70)
- pencil
- colored pencils or markers

Teacher Directions

1. On a strip of construction paper, write "All insects have three body parts and six legs." Laminate the strip and glue a small felt square on the back. Post the strip on a flannel board.
2. Make one copy of *Insect Parts* (page 69). Color the pieces, cut them out, and laminate them. Glue a felt square to the back of each piece and stick the pieces to the flannel board.
3. Place several insect pictures and books near the flannel board.
4. Make a copy of *Insect Inventory* (page 70) for each student.
5. Introduce the center and point out the common characteristics of insects. Give the students the activity page after they have had time to create several insect designs on the flannel board.

Student Directions

1. Study the pictures of insects.
2. Use the felt scraps to make your own insect model. Be sure to cut out a head, thorax, abdomen, and six legs.
3. Display your insect on the flannel board.
4. Tell about your insect on the *Insect Inventory* sheet.

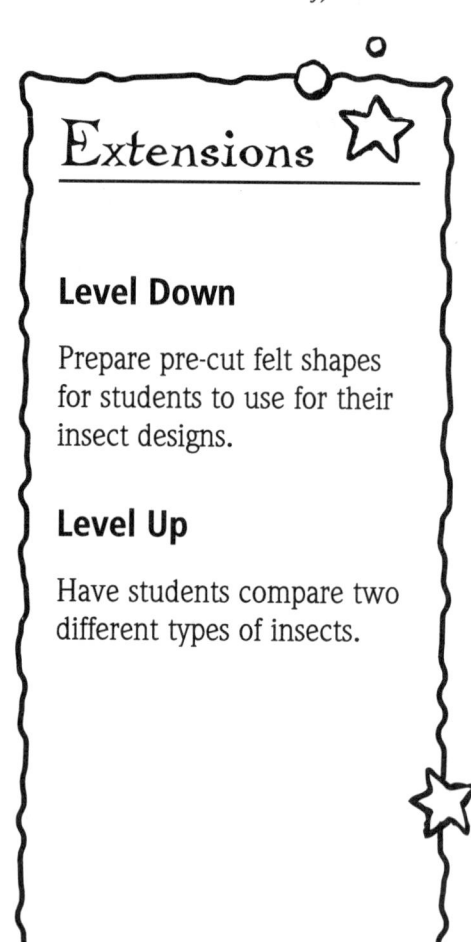

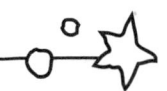

Extensions

Level Down

Prepare pre-cut felt shapes for students to use for their insect designs.

Level Up

Have students compare two different types of insects.

68

© McGraw-Hill Children's Publishing   0-7682-2941-3 *Learning Center Activities for the New Teacher*

Insect Inventory, continued

Insect Parts

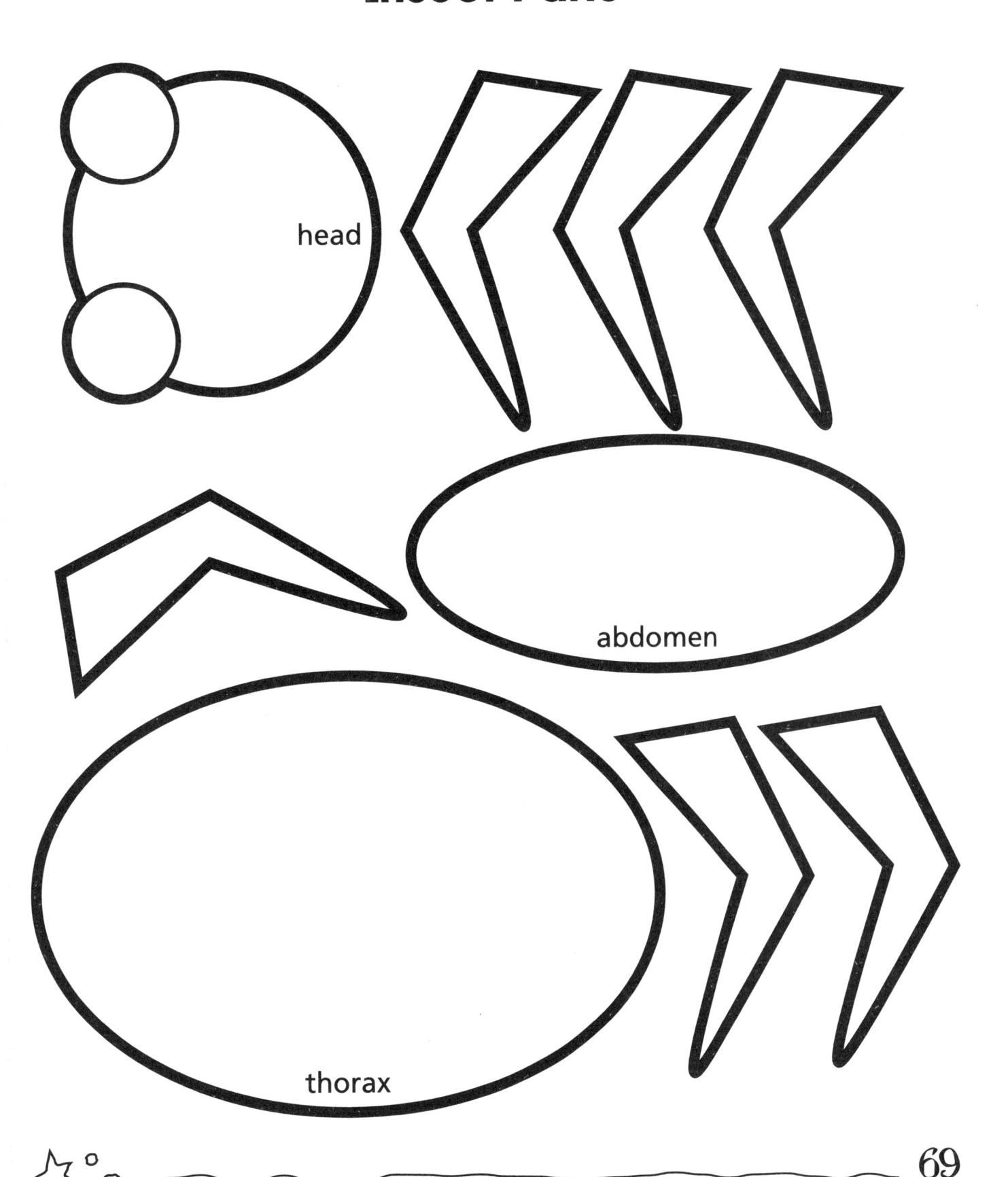

head

abdomen

thorax

Name _____   Date _____

Insect Inventory

Imagine that you have found an insect that no one has ever seen before.

1. Write the name of your insect.

   _____

2. How many legs does your insect have?

   _____

3. How many body parts does your insect have?

   _____

4. Draw a picture of your insect.

Science

What's in the Marsh?

Introduction to the Learning Center

This folder-style center is a quiet introduction to a very important endangered habitat. Marshlands are rich with plant and animal life. Students will discover some marshland inhabitants and gain an appreciation for the environment with this activity.

Skills & Assessment

- Identify plants and animals that live in the marsh
- Assess by having students give "tours" of their marshland pictures.

Tip

Check your school or community library for nature tapes that provide the sounds of a marshland habitat.

Science   *What's in the Marsh?*, continued

Teacher Materials

- portable tape player with earphones
- nature tapes
- pictures of marshland plants and animals
- index card or other label
- glue
- small plastic container labeled "Marsh Plants and Animals"
- picnic basket

Student Materials

- reproducible pages 73 and 74
- scissors
- pencil
- glue
- colored pencils or markers

Teacher Directions

1. Copy pages 73 and 74 for each student. Attach pictures of marshland plants and animals to a picnic basket. Label the basket "What's in the Marsh?"
2. Stock the picnic basket with other materials for the center, including the nature tapes, a tape player, and earphones.
3. Introduce and explain the center.

Student Directions

1. Listen to the nature tapes on the tape player.
2. Color the pictures on both activity sheets.
3. Cut out the pictures on the *Marsh Pictures* page.
4. Glue the pictures over the circles on the *What's in the Marsh?* page.
5. Give a friend a "tour" of your marsh by telling him or her about the pictures.

Extensions

Level Down

Prepare the marsh picture in advance for the students to color as they listen to nature sounds.

Level Up

Have the students draw and label other plants and animals that inhabit marshes.

Name _____   Date _____

What's in the Marsh?

- cattails
- goose
- grass
- fish
- water lily

73

Name _____   Date _____

Marsh Pictures

74
© McGraw-Hill Children's Publishing

0-7682-2941-3 Learning Center Activities for the New Teacher

Science

Standards Correlation:
NAS 2

Exciting Electricity

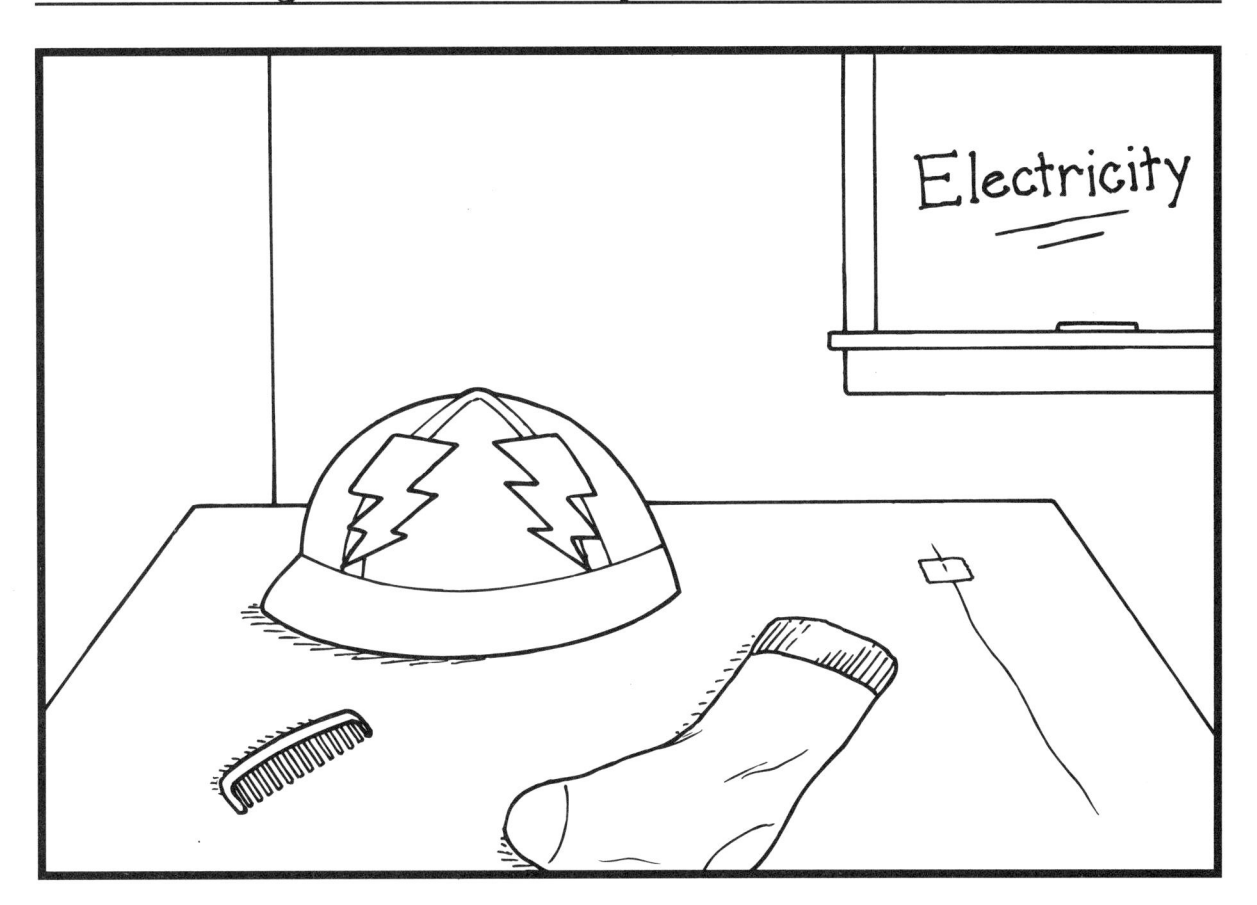

Introduction to the Learning Center

Electricity is all around us. Demonstrate this powerful force through a basic experiment that will peek student interest in scientific inquiries. Plan this activity when an aide or volunteer can assist, but tell your helper to watch out! This activity will make everyone's hair stand on end.

Skills & Assessment

- Identify and create a source of electricity
- Assess by having students report the results of their experiments.

Tip

Help students share the excitement of scientific inquiry. Put all the materials in a paper bag for students to check out and take home. An instruction page for families is included on page 78.

Science   *Exciting Electricity,* continued

Teacher Materials

- yellow construction paper
- scissors
- wool sock
- plastic comb
- one-foot length of lightweight thread
- clear tape
- student-size hard hat

Student Materials

- reproducible page 77

Teacher Directions

1. Cut several lightning bolt shapes out of construction paper. Laminate the shapes and tape them to a hard hat.

2. Tape one end of the thread to the tabletop. Set the wool sock and the comb on the table.

3. Demonstrate static electricity. Rub the sock back and forth rapidly over the comb. Place the comb near your hair to make it stand up. Tell the students that they can make a string stand up, too.

4. Give students a copy of *Experiment* (page 77).

Student Directions

1. Put on your hard hat.
2. Rub the sock back and forth over the comb. Do this very quickly.
3. With the comb, touch the loose end of the thread.
4. Raise the comb into the air.
5. Draw a picture of each step in the experiment on your activity page.

Extensions

Level Down

Have students dictate their sentences to an adult.

Level Up

Have the students experiment with other materials that might stand up for the comb.

76

© McGraw-Hill Children's Publishing   0-7682-2941-3 Learning Center Activities for the New Teacher

Name _____   Date _____

Experiment

Draw a picture to show each step in your experiment.

Step 1	**Step 3**
Step 2	**Step 4**

Finish this sentence:

When I raised the comb into the air, the thread

_____

_____.

Name _____ Date _____

Take-Out Electricity

Follow these steps to create a dazzling electrical experiment for the family.

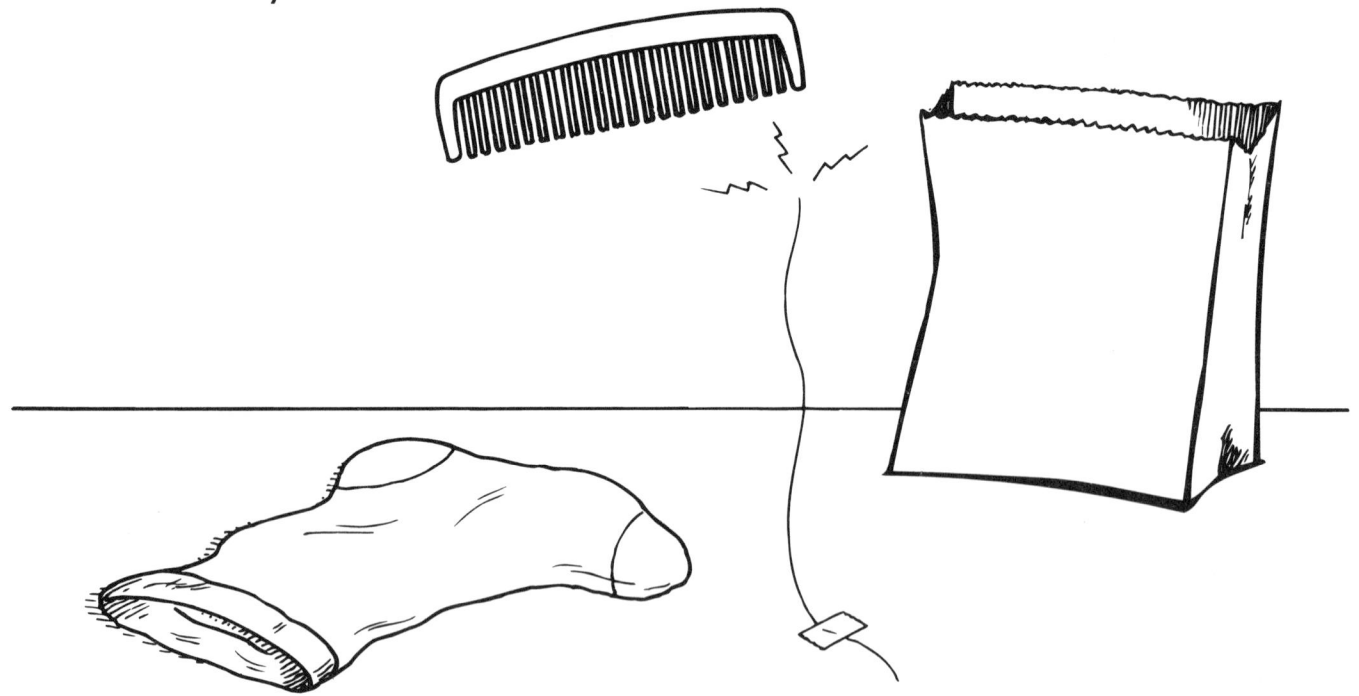

1. Take the materials out of the bag.
2. Tape one end of the thread to the tabletop.
3. Set the wool sock and the comb on the table.
4. Rub the sock back and forth rapidly over the comb.
5. With the comb, touch the loose end of the thread.
6. Raise the comb into the air.
7. Talk about what happened. Can you repeat the experiment with other materials?

Science

Standards Correlation:
AAHE 1, 3; NAS 1, 3

Jumping Germs!

Introduction to the Learning Center

Make every student in the class a germ fighter with this hands-on center. Invite a health care professional to your class to introduce students to Mr. Germ and teach them some important germ-fighting practices. Reward germ-fighting students with a ribbon at the conclusion of the activity.

Skills & Assessment

- Use a microscope to observe germ cells
- Practice disease-prevention strategies
- Assess by having students discuss their observations and recite the "Germ-Fighter Pledge."

Tip

Contact your local medical association or nurses' organization for a health care professional to serve as a classroom volunteer. Such organizations may also be able to lend you microscopes, slides, posters, and literature to share with students.

Science   Jumping Germs!, continued

Teacher Materials

- microscope
- slides of germ cells
- tissue
- soap
- wash basin
- paper towels
- pictures of germs or health posters

Student Materials

- reproducible pages 81 and 82
- pencil
- surgical mask
- eye goggles
- latex gloves

Teacher Directions

1. Gather the materials and set them up in the center. Demonstrate how to use the microscope.

2. Have a health care professional visit your class and discuss the "Germ-Fighter Pledge" with the students. Have students volunteer to act out the points in the pledge.

3. When students have completed the activity, reward each one with the award ribbon on page 82.

Student Directions

1. Work like a scientist! Put on your goggles, mask, and gloves. Then look through the microscope to find germ cells.

2. Read the "Germ-Fighter Pledge."

3. Complete the activity.

4. Practice each of the steps in the pledge.

Extensions

Level Down

Have students sign their names at the bottom of one pledge rather than copying each pledge point.

Level Up

Have students add pledge points that demonstrate good health practices.

Name _____ Date _____

Germ-Fighter Pledge

Read each sentence.
Copy the sentence.
Practice each statement.

1. I will cover my mouth and nose when I sneeze or cough.

   _____

   _____

2. I will use tissue when I blow my nose.

   _____

3. I will wash my hands after using the bathroom.

   _____

   _____

4. I will wash my hands before I eat.

   _____

   _____

Jumping Germs!, continued

Germ-Fighter Award

for

_____

_____

Science

Treasures in the Soil

Introduction to the Learning Center

Sometimes students just need to put their hands in the dirt! Turn this favorite playtime activity into a center for scientific inquiry. Through close analysis, students will discover that soil contains much more than just dirt. This is a perfect outdoor activity.

Skills & Assessment

- Identify objects found in soil
- Assess by having students identify three objects found in the soil samples.

Tip

Tailor your center to reflect the kinds of soils that exist in your area. Your local parks department, greenhouse, or garden store are just a few sources to help you find rich soil samples. If you are brave enough, add some industrious earthworms to the soil.

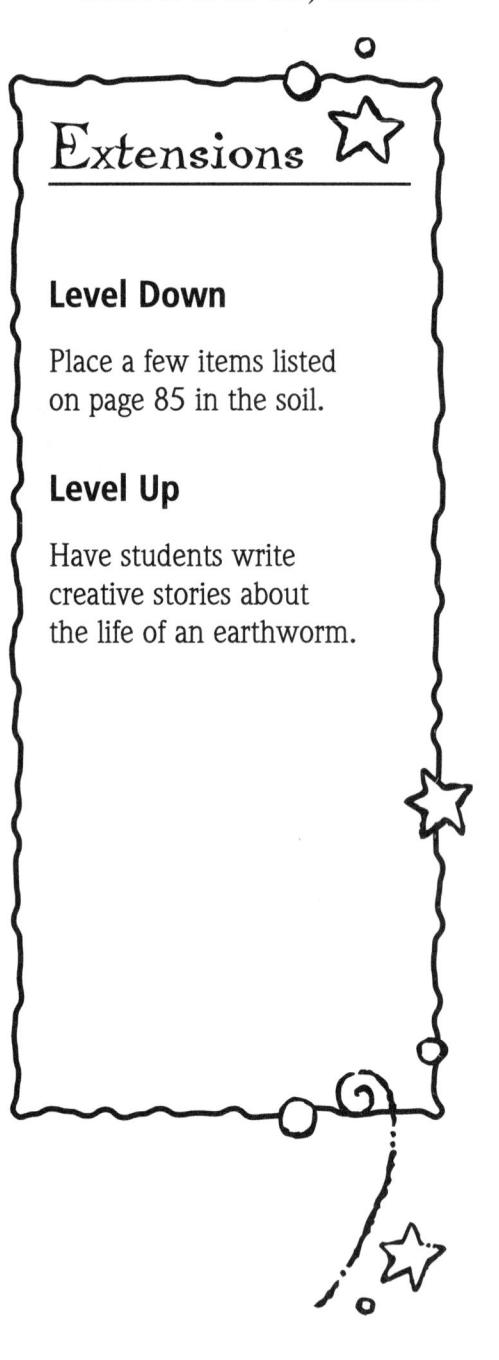

Science   *Treasures in the Soil, continued*

Teacher Materials

- plastic pail or dish tub
- bag of soil
- magnifying glass
- tweezers
- disposable tablecloth
- cardboard tray lined with white paper
- tape
- plastic cup

Student Materials

- one 8-ounce plastic cup
- reproducible pages 85 and 86
- pencil
- colored pencils or markers

Teacher Directions

1. Tape a disposable tablecloth to the floor. Pour some soil into the pail or dish tub. Place the remaining materials on or near the tablecloth.
2. Introduce and explain the center.
3. Give each student a copy of pages 85 and 86.

Student Directions

1. Use a plastic cup to scoop out a sample of soil.
2. Pour your soil sample into the tray.
3. Look at the soil under the magnifying glass.
4. Use the pair of tweezers to pick up things that you find in the soil.
5. Read the directions on your activity pages. Complete the pages.

Extensions

Level Down

Place a few items listed on page 85 in the soil.

Level Up

Have students write creative stories about the life of an earthworm.

Name _____ Date _____

Treasures in the Soil

What did you find in your soil sample?
Check the box if you found:

1. a bug or worm   ☐

2. a stone   ☐

3. a root   ☐

4. seeds   ☐

5. shells   ☐

What else did you find in your soil sample?

6. _____

7. _____

8. _____

Name _____   Date _____

My Soil Sample

Pick an object that you found in your soil sample.
Look at it under the magnifying glass.
Draw a picture of how it looks.

Science

Standards Correlation:
NAS 3

How Old Are You?

Introduction to the Learning Center

How old is a tree? Give students an introduction into the way a tree reveals its age through tree rings. Students will discover that the age of trees, just like people, is not determined by height and diameter, and they'll be able to create trees to match their own age.

Skills & Assessment

- Count tree rings to determine a tree's age
- Assess by having students tell you the age of each tree stump displayed in the center.

Tip

A local forestry department or landscaping facility is a good source for locating trunks for the center display.

Science   How Old Are You?, continued

Teacher Materials

- several small tree stumps
- photographs of trees

Student Materials

- reproducible pages 89 and 90
- pencil
- colored pencils or markers

Teacher Directions

1. Set up and introduce the center.
2. Assist the students in counting the rings on each trunk sample.
3. Give each student a copy of pages 89 and 90.

Student Directions

1. Look at the tree stumps in the center.
2. Count the rings on each stump to find out how old the tree is.
3. Follow the instructions on the activity pages.

Extensions

Level Down

Give students only one activity page to complete.

Level Up

Introduce tree-related terms, such as *bark, wood, sapwood,* and *heartwood.*

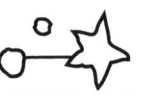

Name _____ Date _____

How Old Are You?

Count the rings on the tree trunk. Write your answer to complete the sentence.

This tree trunk is _____ years old.

89

© McGraw-Hill Children's Publishing   0-7682-2941-3 Learning Center Activities for the New Teacher

Name _____ Date _____

A Tree as Old as Me

Draw a tree stump that is the same age you are.

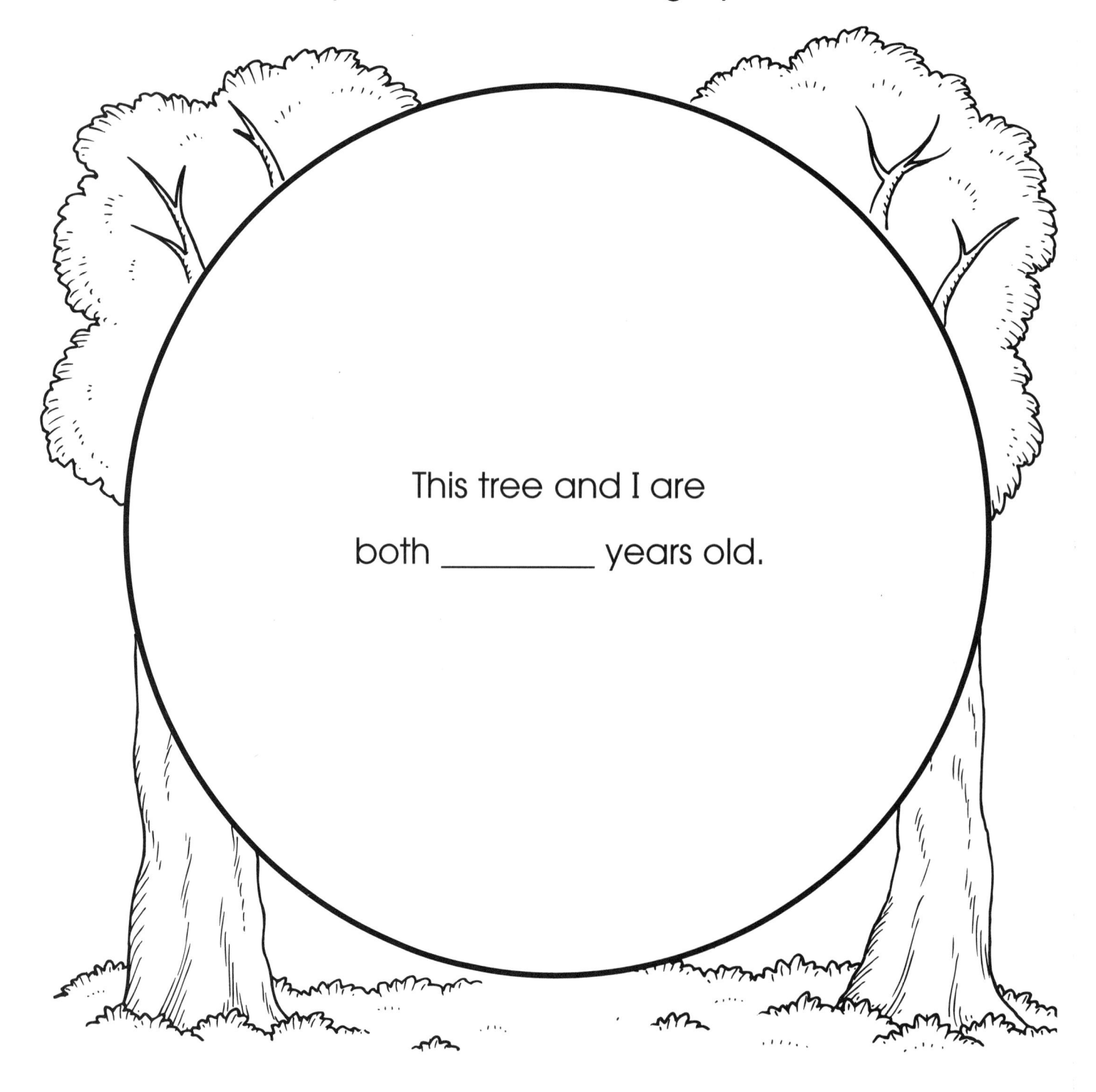

This tree and I are both _____ years old.

90

Science   Standards Correlation:
NAS 1, 2, 6

Wheels Make the World Go Round

Introduction to the Learning Center

The wheel was invented around 3,500 B.C., and it remains one of the greatest inventions of all time. In this hands-on center, students will build models of water wheels like those used to power grist mills and sawmills. Implement this center on a day when a volunteer can assist in the classroom.

Skills & Assessment

- Understand the use of wheels in daily life
- Make a water wheel
- Assess by having the class make a list of wheels and their uses.

Tip

Contact your local or state historical society to obtain information on water wheels used in your region. Many of these organizations have brochures, photographs, and videos of the wheels at work.

Teacher Materials

- pictures of water wheels
- objects with wheels (rolling pin, roller skates, bicycle, yo-yo)
- one round plastic food lid
- one pencil
- two thick rubber bands
- access to water faucet
- reproducible pages 93 and 94

91

© McGraw-Hill Children's Publishing   0-7682-2941-3 Learning Center Activities for the New Teacher

Science   Wheels Make the World Go Round, continued

Student Materials

- one round plastic food lid
- one pencil
- two thick rubber bands
- access to water faucet

Teacher Directions

1. Display your collection of objects with wheels. Show the students pictures of various water wheels.
2. Punch a hole in the center of each plastic lid.
3. Follow the student directions below to make a sample water wheel.
4. Set up and explain the center.

Student Directions

1. Take one plastic lid. Cut slits around the edge of the lid. The slits should be about three finger-lengths apart. Do not cut all the way to the center.
2. Bend every other section of the lid up. Bend the other sections down.
3. Push a pencil through the middle of the lid. Make sure the hole is big enough so that the lid can spin around the pencil.
4. Wrap a rubber band around each end of the pencil to hold it in place. Push the rubber bands toward the center of the lid.
5. Have a partner hold the pencil at each end.
6. Turn the water faucet on so that the water is running slowly.
7. Put the wings of the water wheel under the water tap.
8. Watch the wheel spin around.
9. Open the water faucet more. Watch the wheel spin faster.
10. Complete the activity pages.

Extensions

Level Down

Prepare the water wheel models ahead of time for the students.

Level Up

Challenge students to find several uses for their water wheel.

© McGraw-Hill Children's Publishing   0-7682-2941-3 Learning Center Activities for the New Teacher

Name _____   Date _____

Water Wheel

Color the picture.

What do you think this wheel is used for?

_____

93

Name _____ Date _____

Wheel Web

Draw a picture of a different kind of wheel in each large circle. Write one way the wheel is used in the oval.

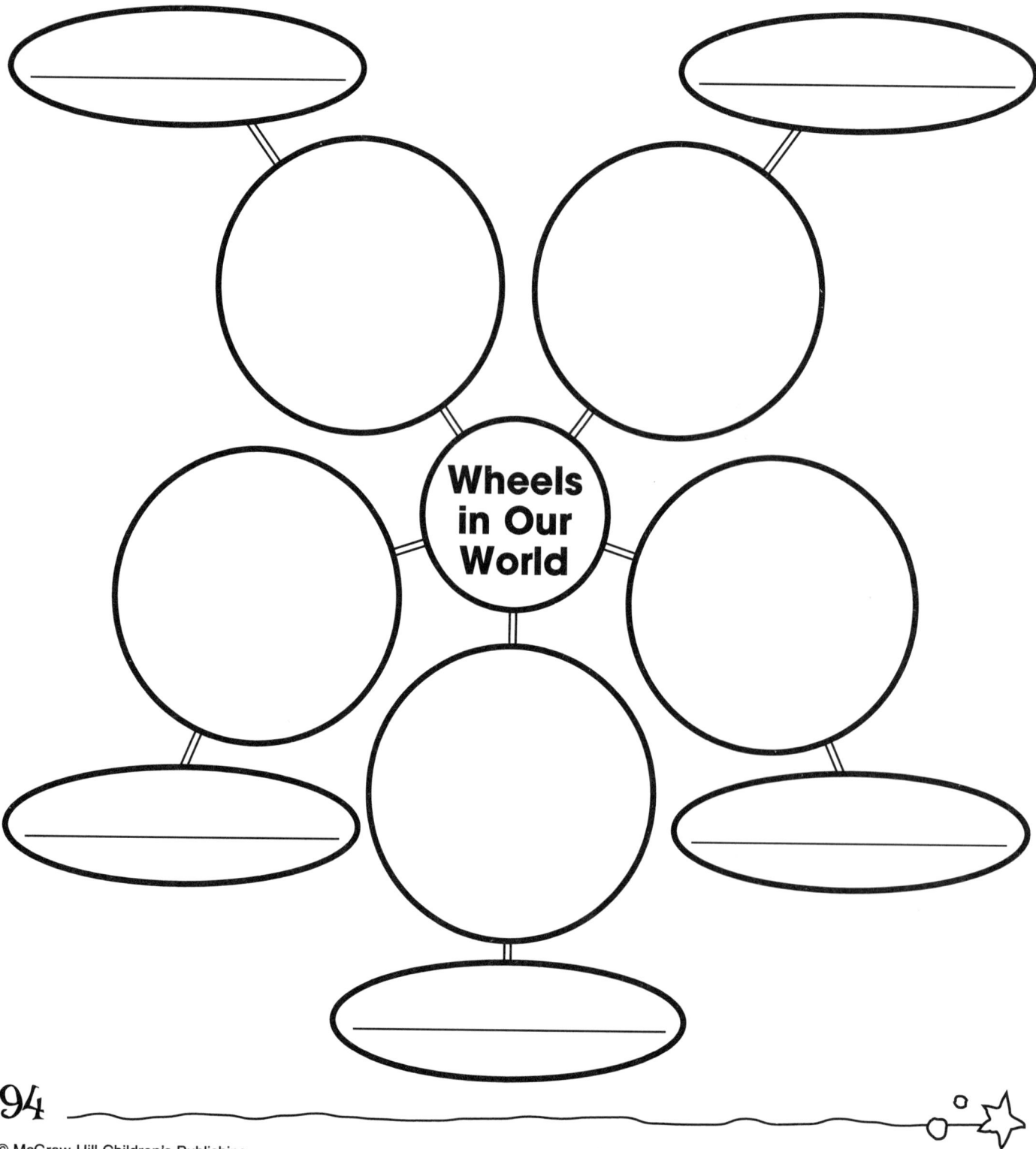

Wheels in Our World

94

© McGraw-Hill Children's Publishing

0-7682-2941-3 Learning Center Activities for the New Teacher

Social Studies

Standards Correlation:
NCSS U.S. History 1, 3

Log Cabin Days

Introduction to the Learning Center

Give students a taste of the chores performed by children of yesteryear. This outdoor hands-on center introduces students to the work that made up daily life in the 19th century. This center is a great follow-up to stories by Laura Ingalls Wilder or other stories about frontier life.

Skills & Assessment

- Complete daily chores similar to those of a 19th century child
- Assess by having students compare the chores with those that they complete today.

Tip

Invite parents, grandparents, and great-grandparents to share in this adventure to enrich the multi-generational learning experience.

Social Studies *Log Cabin Days, continued*

Teacher Materials:

- dried corn on the cob
- two large circular plastic wash tubs
- life-size baby doll with clothing
- doll-size baby crib with blankets
- baby bottle
- washboard
- clothesline
- clothespins
- several old T-shirts
- several sticks of fireplace wood
- *Certificate* (page 98) for each student
- *Signs* (page 97), enlarged
- wooden stakes to hold the signs
- glue

Student Materials

- none

Teacher Directions

1. Reproduce each sign shown on page 97 onto tagboard. Glue each sign to a wooden stake. Post each stake by its station.
2. Place corn in one large wash basin.
3. Place the doll and bottle in the crib.
4. Place T-shirts in the second wash tub with the washboard. Hang the clothesline nearby. Pin the clothespins to the line.
5. Stack the wood in a pile.
6. Introduce each station.

Student Directions

Follow the directions at each station.

Extensions

Level Down

Set up only one station at a time.

Level Up

Add stations for writing with a quill pen, making butter, making hard tack, and carrying water.

Log Cabin Days, *continued*

Signs

Tend the Baby

1. Watch the baby at all times.
2. Hold the baby when she cries.
3. Feed the baby.

Shell Corn

Use your fingers to remove the corn from the cob.

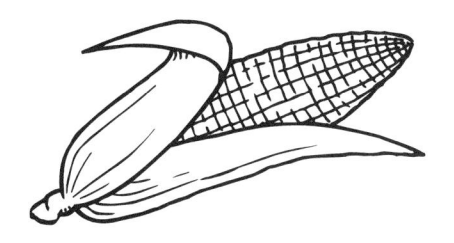

Wash Clothes

1. Fill the tub halfway with water.
2. Dunk one T-shirt at a time into the water.
3. Scrub the T-shirt on the board.
4. Wring out the T-shirt.
5. Hang the T-shirt on the clothesline to dry.

Carry Wood

1. Pick up a load of wood.
2. Carry it to the baby's crib.
3. Carry it back to the wood pile.

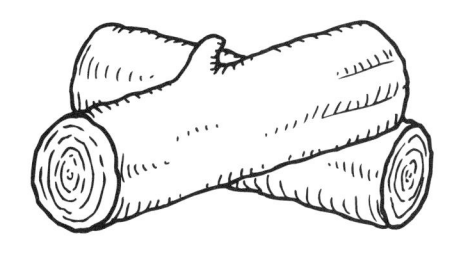

Log Cabin Days, continued

Certificate

This is to certify that

_____

has completed
these chores of yesteryear:

shelling corn
tending the baby
carrying wood
washing clothes

during Log Cabin Days at our school.

_____   _____
Date   Teacher

_____
Name of School

Social Studies   Standards Correlation:
                                             NCSS U.S. History 1

All in the Family

Introduction to the Learning Center

For centuries, many families designed crests to tell about themselves and to identify their members. This historic center gives students a glimpse of the past and helps them design their own unique family crests.

Skills & Assessment

- Create a crest design that symbolizes one's family
- Assess by having students give oral presentations to explain their designs.

Tip

Historical societies and genealogical groups may be able to lend you pictures or books that feature family crests. If not, see if your local library has any books available on crest designs.

Students who are unfamiliar with their family backgrounds can make crests based on their own personal interests.

Social Studies — *All in the Family, continued*

Teacher Materials:

- samples of crest designs
- world maps or a globe
- colored pencils, markers, or crayons

Student Materials

- reproducible pages 101 and 102
- pencil
- colored pencils, markers, or crayons

Teacher Directions

1. Design a sample crest to display in the center.
2. Set up and introduce the center. Explain to the students that a family crest uses pictures to tell about the family. People can use a crest to help identify the members of the family.
3. Give each student a copy of reproducible pages 101 and 102. Let the students use maps and globes to locate where their ancestors lived. Encourage the students to study the pictures of family crests that are available.
4. When all of the students have completed their designs, ask each student to present his or her crest to the class.

Student Directions

1. Think about your family. Answer the questions on the *About My Family* activity page.
2. Use the information from your *About My Family* page to design a crest. Draw your crest on the *My Family Crest* page.
3. Show your crest to the class. Explain what each picture means.

Extensions

Level Down

Work in small groups with students to help them come up with symbols that tell about their families' values.

Level Up

Have students take their crest designs home and work with their families to write stories about their ancestors.

Name _____ Date _____

About My Family

Think about your family. Where did your family come from? What is important to your family? Answer the questions below.

Ancestors are people in our families who lived long, long ago. In what country did your ancestors live? _____

Think of a picture that would remind people of that place. Draw your picture here.

List three things that are important to your family. Draw a picture to remind people of each one.

_____

_____

_____

Use your pictures to help you make a crest for your family.

Name _____ Date _____

My Family Crest

Social Studies   *Standards Correlation:*
NCSS Science, Technology, and Society 1, 2

A Few of My Favorites

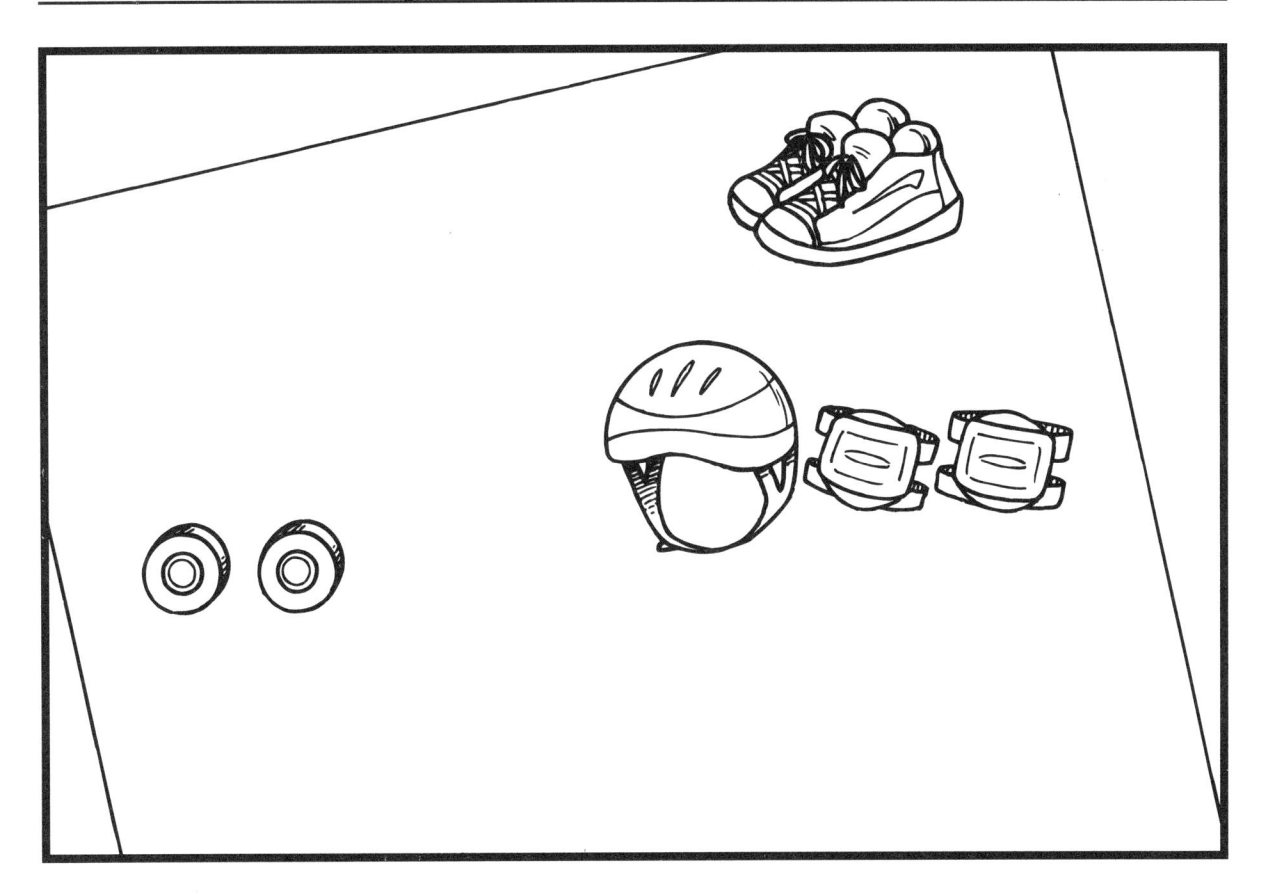

Introduction to the Learning Center

In this center, students will begin to understand the interdependence between their favorite activities and the inventions needed in order to participate in the activities. Students will create simple rebus pictures to illustrate what they've learned.

Skills & Assessment

- Identify inventions that have an impact on daily life
- Assess by having students read their rebus stories to the class.

Tip

Look through the comic section of your local newspaper to find printed samples of rebus stories to share with the students.

Social Studies	*A Few of My Favorites!*, continued

Teacher Materials

- several objects of interest to students, such as sports equipment, books, various toys, and pictures of favorite places
- strip of construction paper
- scissors
- glue
- samples of rebus stories
- reproducible pages 105 and 106

Student Materials

- reproducible pages 105 and 106
- sheet of construction paper
- scissors
- glue

Teacher Directions

1. Use your strip of construction paper to make a sample rebus story. Show a favorite activity that requires the use of different inventions. Use this story frame for your sample: *If I didn't have _____, _____, and _____, I couldn't _____.*
2. Put the objects of interest in the center, along with several samples of rebus stories.
3. Copy pages 105 and 106 for each student.
4. Talk with the students about their favorite activities. Have the students identify various inventions that are needed in order for them to participate in the activities.
5. Display your sample rebus story and explain the directions for the center.

Student Directions

1. Draw a picture of one of your favorite activities in the circle on the *Favorite Things* page.
2. On your *Inventions* page, draw a picture in each box that shows something you need to participate in the activity.
3. Cut out the circle and the three boxes.
4. Write *If I didn't have* on your sheet of construction paper. Glue the three boxes in a row after that. Then write *I couldn't* and glue the circle to the construction paper after that.

Extensions

Level Down

Have the students identify only one invention needed for each activity.

Level Up

Have the students write stories about their favorite activities.

Name _____ Date _____

Favorite Things

Draw a picture in the circle of one of your favorite activities.

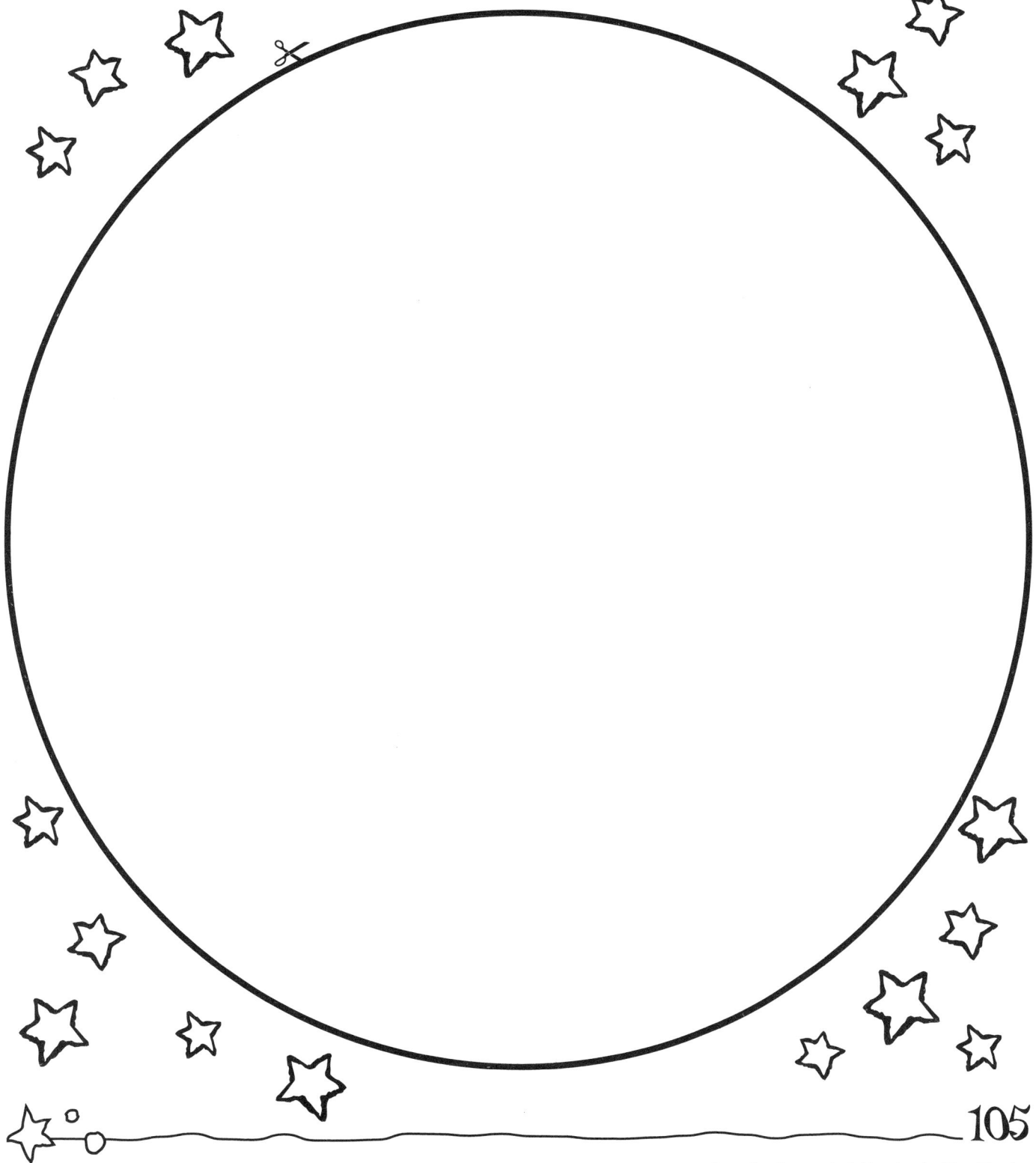

105

© McGraw-Hill Children's Publishing

0-7682-2941-3 *Learning Center Activities for the New Teacher*

Name _____   Date _____

Inventions

Draw a picture in each box that shows something you need to do your favorite activity.

Social Studies

The Other Side

Introduction to the Learning Center

The world is a very small place, and this message comes home for students when they look at who lives on the other side of the globe. This center combines a hands-on lesson in geography and culture, as students find out there is someone awake on the other side of the world when they are sleeping.

Skills & Assessment

- Identify and appreciate another country
- Assess by having student locate and name the country without assistance.

Tip

Use Internet resources to contact the ambassador to the country selected by students. Many exchange programs exist so that students can send and receive correspondence with a school from that country.

Also check Web sites and online encyclopedias for additional information on the country. Students will enjoy seeing photos of children from the selected country.

Social Studies   The Other Side, *continued*

Teacher Materials

- world globe
- table lamp with adjustable light
- self-adhesive notes

Student Materials

- reproducible pages 109 and 110
- pencil
- colored pencils or markers

Teacher Directions

1. Set up and introduce the center.
2. Mark the students' home on the globe with a self-adhesive note. Place another note on the opposite side of the globe.
3. Turn on the light so that it shines directly on the place where the student lives.
4. Let students turn the globe until the other sticky note is directly under the light.
5. Help students identify the country before handing out the reproducible pages.

Student Directions

Follow the directions on your activity pages.

Extensions:

Level Down

Draw the outline map of the country for students to color.

Level Up

Have students read books about life in the selected country.

Name _____ Date _____

The Other Side

Draw a picture of the country that is on the other side of the world from you.

Write the name of the country on the picture.
Color the country.

109

Name _____   Date _____

My Home

Follow the directions to complete the letter.

Dear Friend:

I know where you live. I live on the opposite side of the world from you. When I am sleeping, you are awake.
When you are sleeping, I am in school.

This is a picture of my country:

I have put an X where I live.
I hope that we can meet someday.

Sincerely,

_____
name

_____
street address

_____
city

_____
state

_____
zip code

_____
country

Social Studies
Standards Correlation:
NCSS Geography 2, 5

What Did You Say?

Introduction to the Learning Center

Imagine being in a place where you do not speak the language. Help students learn to use gestures to communicate with a teammate in this folder-style instant center.

Skills & Assessment:

- Understand an alternative way to communicate
- Assess by having students demonstrate non-verbal communication for another class.

Tip

Make additional flash cards to use in this center by writing familiar words on index cards.

Social Studies   *What Did You Say?*, continued

Teacher Materials

- reproducible pages 113 and 114
- 3" x 5" card file box labeled, "What Did You Say?"

Student Materials

- none

Teacher Directions

1. Copy reproducible pages 113 and 114. Cut out and laminate the cards.
2. Place the cards in the box.
3. Introduce and explain the center.
4. Select teams of two.

Student Directions

1. Take turns drawing cards.
2. The first player takes a card.
3. Don't show the card to your teammate.
4. Without speaking, use hand gestures to describe the word on the card.
5. Continue until your teammate guesses the word.
6. Remember, no talking!

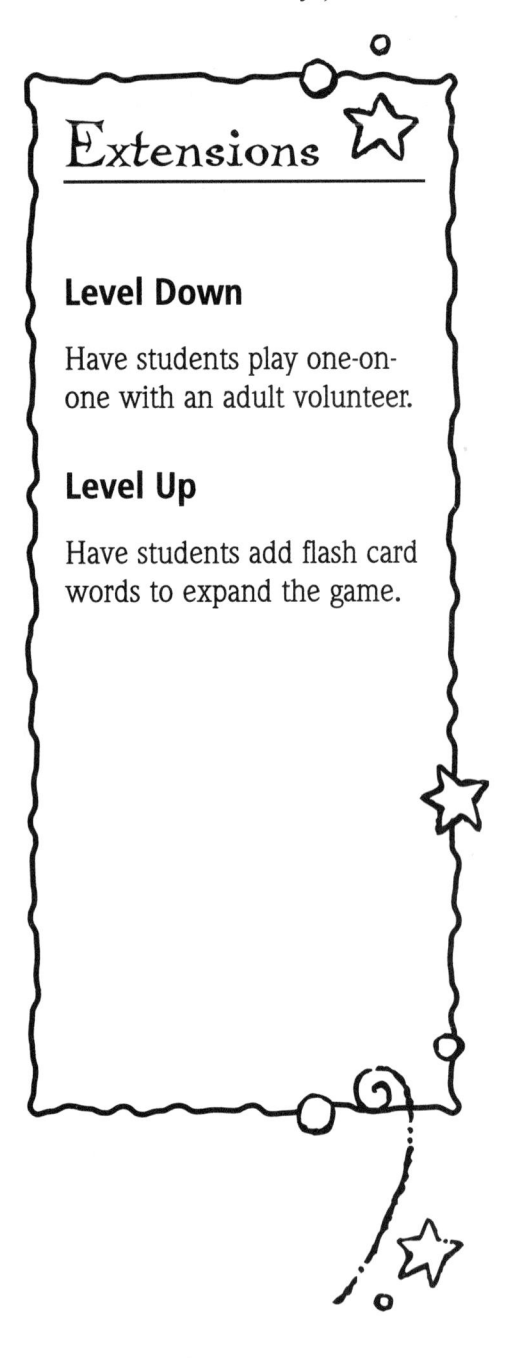

Extensions

Level Down

Have students play one-on-one with an adult volunteer.

Level Up

Have students add flash card words to expand the game.

What Did You Say?, continued

sad	happy
loud	quiet

What Did You Say?, continued

night	day
stop	**walk**

Social Studies

My Room

Introduction to the Learning Center

Everyone has to make decisions. Help students tackle the process of decision making as they plan and design their very own bedrooms.

Skills & Assessment

- Make choices based on needs and wants
- Assess by having students describe how they determined what was a need versus what was a want.

Tip

Expand the center with a math activity. Have students use non-standard measurement tools to measure the size of their rooms.

Social Studies *My Room, continued*

Teacher Materials

- child's cot or board supported by two crates
- pillow
- bedspread
- small lamp
- small table
- children's books
- small bookshelf
- basket of toys

Student Materials

- reproducible pages 117 and 118
- scissors
- glue
- colored pencils or markers

Teacher Directions

1. Set up a mock bedroom in the center similar to the illustration on *My Room* (page 117). The room should be very tiny.
2. Introduce the center and provide examples of needs and wants.
3. Select teams of two to arrange the room with all the furnishings; emphasize that they cannot make the room larger.
4. Have the students remove all the items they do not need.
5. Give each student a copy of pages 117 and 118. Explain the directions.

Student Directions

1. Look at the *Furnishings* page.
2. Cut out the pictures of things that you need in your room.
3. Glue them onto the *My Room* page.
4. Cut out the pictures of things that you would like in your room.
5. Decide which ones will fit in the room.
6. Glue these pictures onto the *My Room* page.
7. Color your room picture.

Extensions

Level Down

Have the students arrange only the items in the mock bedroom.

Level Up

Have students design other rooms in a house such as the living room and the kitchen. Have them base their designs on needs and wants.

My Room

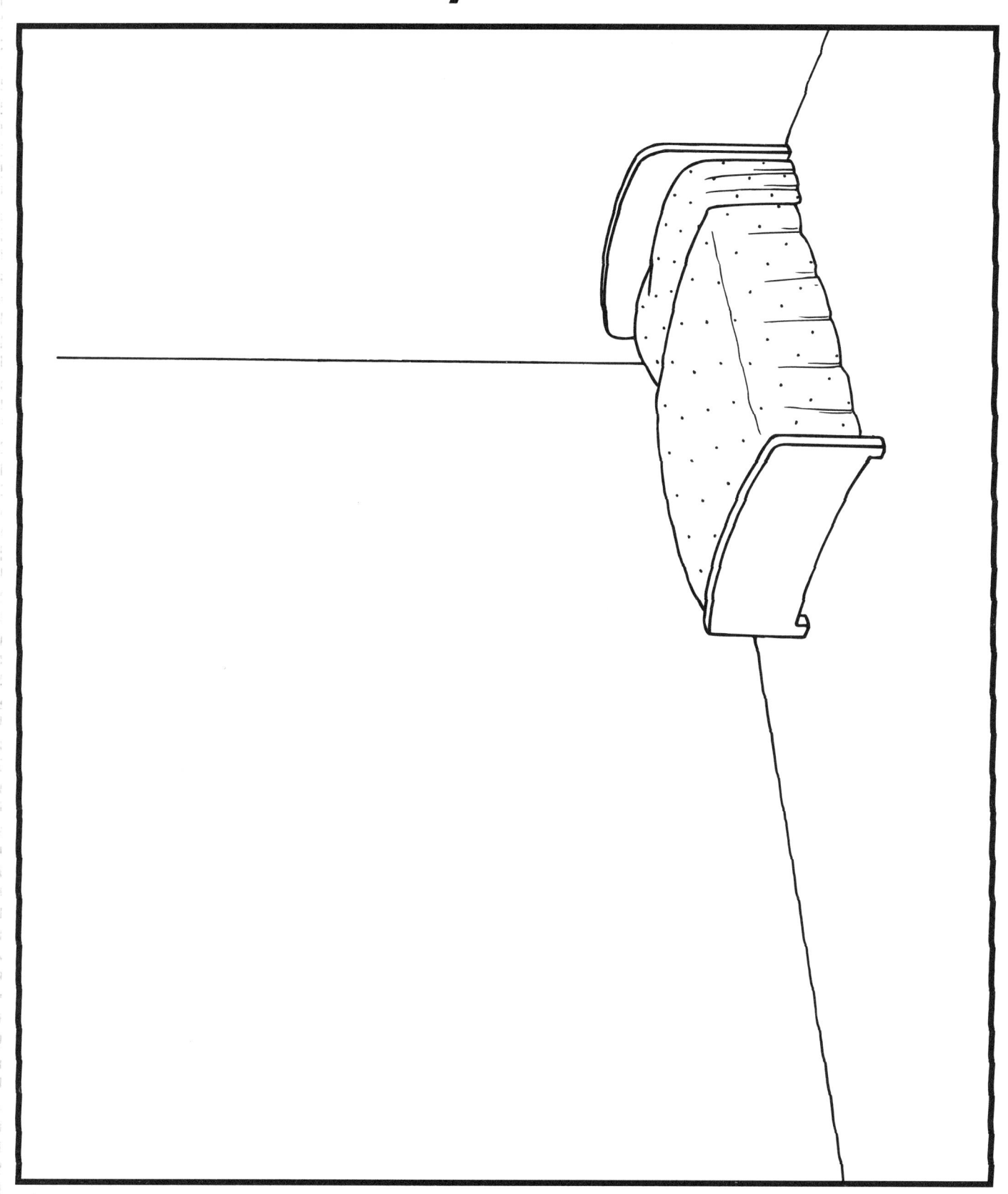

117

My Room, continued

Furnishings

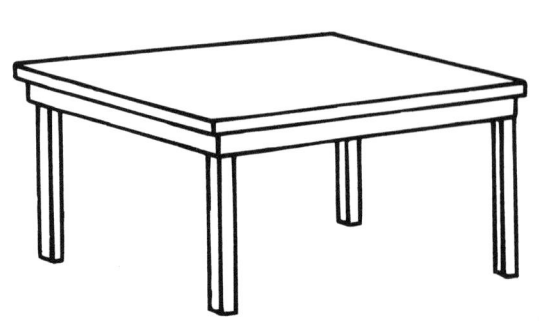

118

Music

Lively Listening

Introduction to the Learning Center

Students will learn through music and movement in this simple center. By joining in a chant, the students will hone their listening skills, practice using sound patterns, and develop a sense of rhythm.

Skills & Assessment

- Create a rhythmic pattern
- Follow musical cues
- Assess by having students perform the chant for others.

Tip

If noise level is a concern, consider moving this center outside or to a music room.

Music   Lively Listening, continued

Teacher Materials

- reproducible pages 121 and 122

Student Materials

- reproducible pages 121 and 122

Teacher Directions

1. Review the "Follow Me" chant.
2. Perform one reading without the students.
3. Perform additional readings, giving the students cues during the performance.

Student Directions

1. Listen to your teacher read the "Follow Me" chant aloud.
2. Watch your teacher's movements and copy what he or she does.
3. Practice saying the chant with your teacher.

Extensions

Level Down

Complete only one verse of the music.

Level Up

Have students make musical instruments out of simple materials. Have them use the instruments to accompany the chant.

Lively Listening, continued

Follow Me

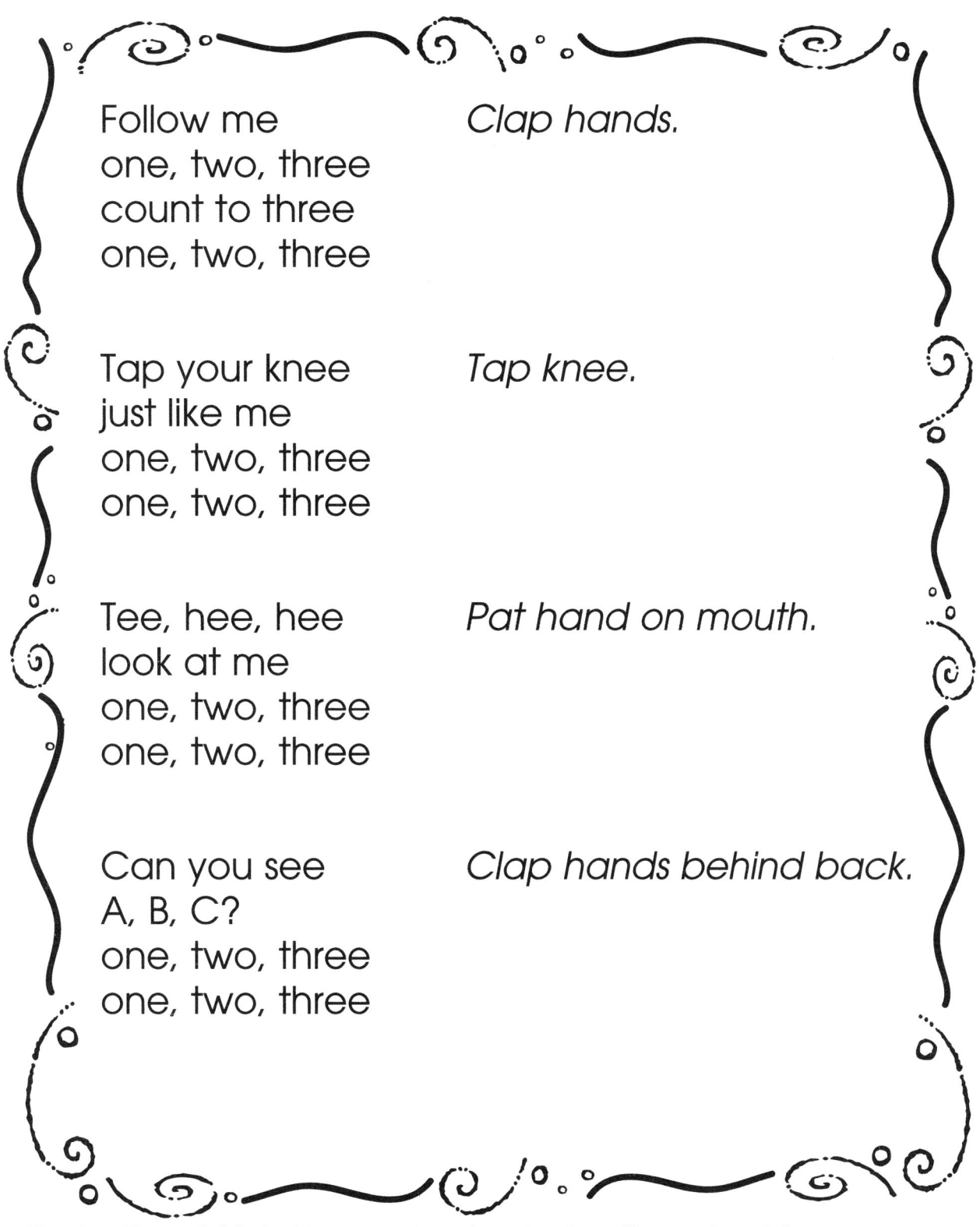

Follow me
one, two, three
count to three
one, two, three

Clap hands.

Tap your knee
just like me
one, two, three
one, two, three

Tap knee.

Tee, hee, hee
look at me
one, two, three
one, two, three

Pat hand on mouth.

Can you see
A, B, C?
one, two, three
one, two, three

Clap hands behind back.

Teacher: Keep a 1-2-3 rhythm pattern throughout the chant. Have students follow your gestures. Have students join in speaking every time they hear the words *one, two, three*.

Lively Listening, continued

Follow Me (continued)

Tum, tum, tum
oh, what fun
say three, two, one
three, two, one

Pat hands on ears.

Now we're done
got to run
three, two, one
three, two, one

Put finger up to lips in gesture to be quiet.

Stand by me
like a tree
one, two, three
one, two, three

Get more and more quiet.

Let's sit down
on the ground

Slow down rhythm as you slowly sit down on floor.

one, two, three
one, two, three

Whisper.

one, two, three
one, two, three

Fade away.

Music

A Song by Me

Introduction to the Learning Center

Create a room of composers with this hands-on keyboard center. Students will learn about musical scales and notes as they compose their own simple tunes.

Skills & Assessment

- Identify notes in a musical scale
- Create a musical composition
- Assess by having each student play his or her composition for the class.

Tip

Invite students who play musical instruments to perform a song for the class.

Music   A Song by Me, continued

Teacher Materials

- keyboard
- earphones
- ten labels for keyboard keys: a, b, c, d, e, f, g, a, b, c

Student Materials

- reproducible pages 125 and 126
- pencil

Teacher Directions

1. Label the keys on a keyboard as shown in the illustration on page 125.
2. Introduce the center by playing scales and simple tunes that use the notes labeled.
3. Give each student the opportunity to play labeled notes on the keyboard.
4. Give each student a copy of pages 125 and 126.

Student Directions

1. Look at the letters on the keyboard.
2. Make up a song using the keys that have letters on them.
3. Write each letter of your song in the blanks on your activity page.
4. After all the blanks are filled in, play the song you wrote on the keyboard for your classmates.
5. Color the picture of the keyboard.

Extensions

Level Down

Fill in the notes on page 126 for the students to play.

Level Up

Give students an extra song page for longer compositions.

Name _____ Date _____

Keyboard

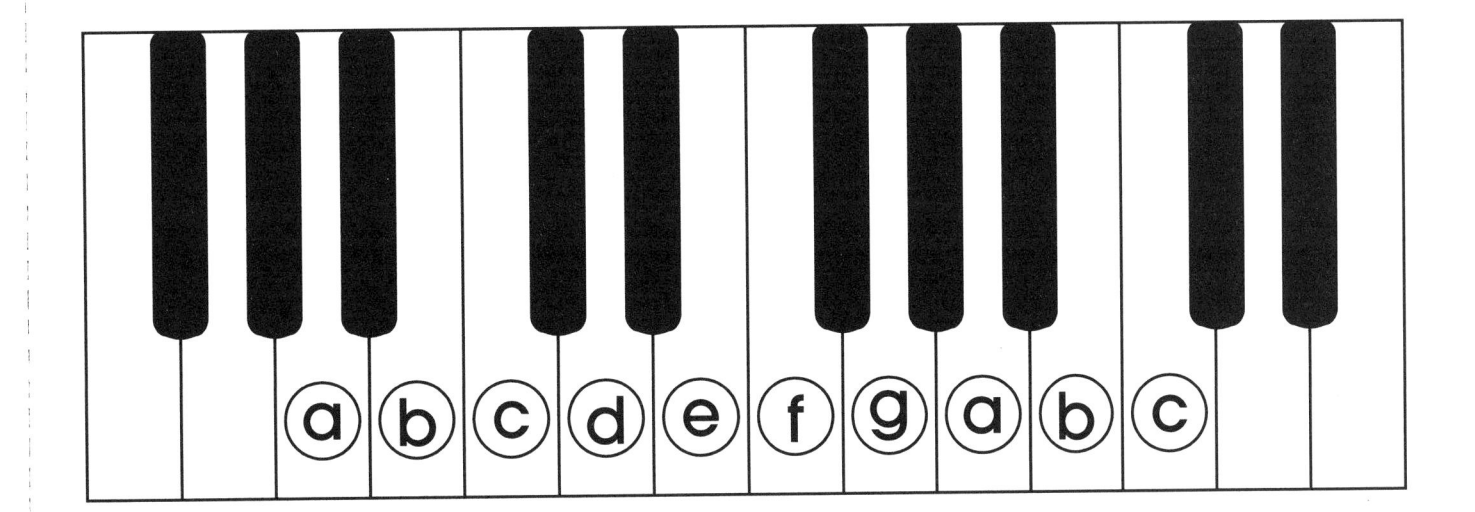

a b c d e f g a b c

Name _____ Date _____

My Own Song

Music/Art

Standards Correlation:
MENC Music 1, 8; Visual Arts 1, 6

A Rainbow Rhyme

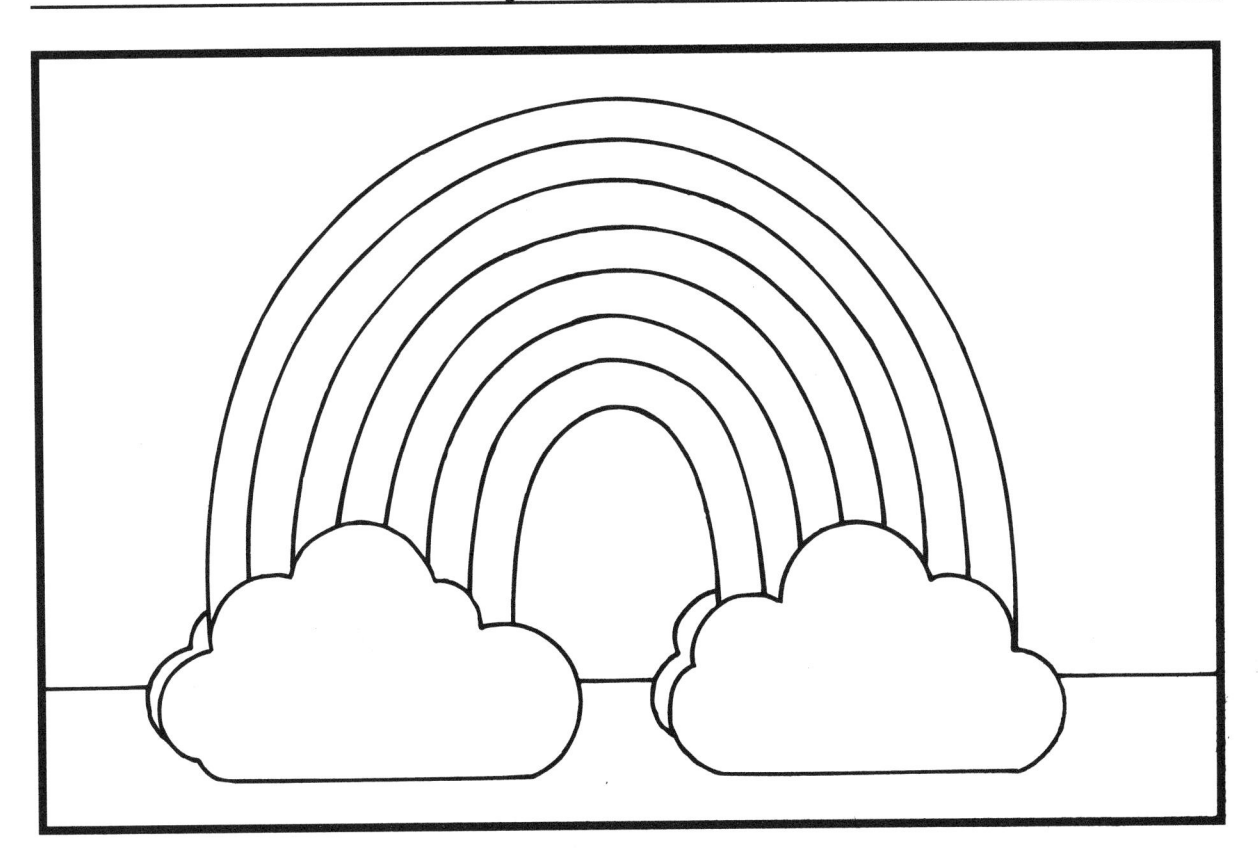

Introduction to the Learning Center

In this center, students will learn the order of the colors in a rainbow. A simple song will help them memorize the information.

Skills & Assessment

- Sing along with a familiar tune
- Create artwork based on a song
- Assess by having students identify the colors on various pictures of rainbows.

Tip

Hold a sing-along for the entire class with a medley of songs about rainbows.

Music/Art

A Rainbow Rhyme, *continued*

Teacher Materials

- cardboard
- paint or marker in these colors—red, orange, yellow, green, blue, indigo, and violet
- two large pieces of white paper
- four heavy bookends
- white tissue paper
- reproducible page 129

Student Materials

- reproducible pages 129 and 130
- colored pencils or markers

Teacher Directions

1. Make a rainbow display for the center. Draw a large rainbow shape on a piece of cardboard. Cut it out and trace it on two sheets of white paper. Draw seven arcs on each sheet of white paper. Paint the arcs in this order, starting from the top—red, orange, yellow, green, blue, indigo, violet. Tape one arc to each side of the cardboard. Stand the rainbow upright and anchor it in place with two bookends on each side. Cover bookends with white tissue paper to make them look like clouds.

2. Introduce the center and sing the song with the students, pointing out the colors each time they are mentioned in the song.

3. Give each student *Rainbow Rhyme* (page 130) to complete.

Student Directions

1. Sing the "Rainbow Song" with your group.
2. Color the rainbow on your activity sheet.

Extensions

Level Down

Write the names of the colors on the *Rainbow Rhyme* page.

Level Up

Have students memorize the "Rainbow Song."

A Rainbow Rhyme, continued

Rainbow Song
(sing to the tune of "Twinkle, Twinkle, Little Star")

Pretty rainbow in the sky
Seven colors up so high.

Red

Orange

I can name each one for you.
Red is first, then orange, it's true.

Yellow

Yellow follows next in line.
Then green and blue, just as fine.

Green

Blue

Indigo and violet rest
At the bottom where it's best.

Indigo

Pretty rainbow in the sky
Seven colors up so high.

Violet

129

Name _____ Date _____

Rainbow Rhyme

130
© McGraw-Hill Children's Publishing

0-7682-2941-3 Learning Center Activities for the New Teacher

Art

Glorious Glass

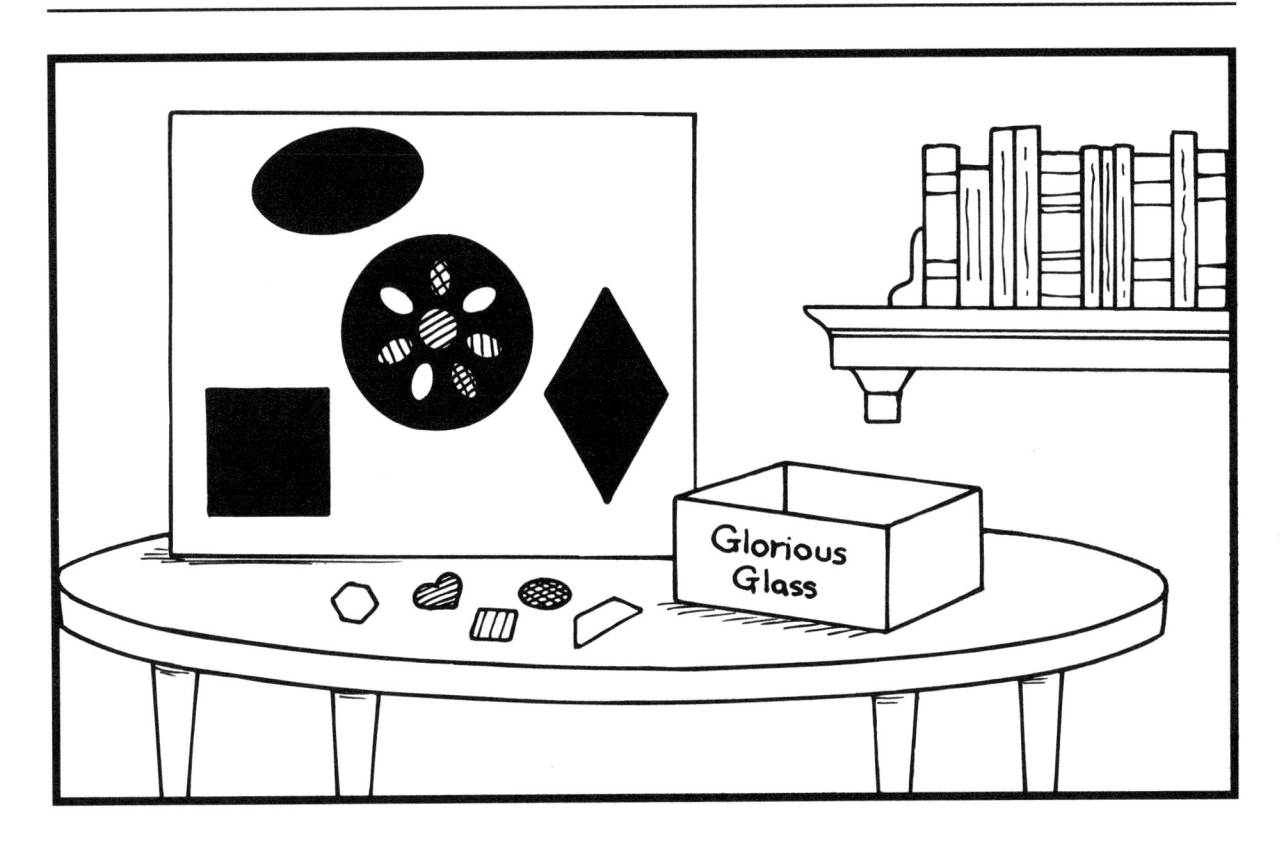

Introduction to the Learning Center

Students will experiment with colors, shapes, and patterns in this creative introduction to stained glass. They will enjoy designing and creating their own "stained glass" projects that reflect the art form that dates back to ancient Egypt.

Skills & Assessment

- Use colors, shapes, and patterns to design a "stained glass" window
- Assess by having students display their projects and describe the elements they used to create them.

Tip

Ask your librarian or media specialist for a selection of books containing examples of both traditional and modern stained glass.

Art   *Glorious Glass, continued*

Teacher Materials

- reproducible pages 133 and 134
- samples of stained glass art
- flannel board
- felt in a variety of colors, including black
- scissors
- shoe box

Student Materials

- reproducible pages 133 and 134
- scissors
- glue
- construction paper in a variety of colors

Teacher Directions

1. Cut these large shapes from black felt—oval, circle, square, and diamond. Place the shapes on the flannel board.

2. Copy the patterns on pages 133 and 134. Cut them out and trace them onto pieces of colored felt. Cut out the felt pieces and place them in a shoe box in the center.

3. Introduce the center. Model how to create designs on the flannel board using the shapes. Talk about stained glass with the students and show them several examples in books.

4. After the students have had an opportunity to create several of their own designs on the flannel board, have them use paper shapes and glue to make a permanent piece of "stained glass" art.

Student Directions

1. Use the colored shapes to make designs on the black oval, circle, square, and diamond. Find the colors you would like to use for your window.

2. Pick a design that you like. Use the patterns on your activity sheets to trace the shapes onto colored pieces of construction paper.

3. When you have decided where each piece should be placed, glue it onto a larger piece of shaped construction paper.

Extensions

Level Down

Create a sample design for the students to copy.

Level Up

Let students create multiple designs.

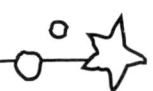

Name _____ Date _____

Glorious Glass Patterns

133

Name _____ Date _____

Glorious Glass Patterns

134

© McGraw-Hill Children's Publishing

0-7682-2941-3 *Learning Center Activities for the New Teacher*

Art

Standards Correlation:
MENC Visual Arts 1, 4

Keepsake Memories

Introduction to the Learning Center

Long before photographs, people drew silhouettes to create images of others that they wanted to remember. This multi-generational center is a great hands-on activity for a Grandparents' Day celebration.

Skills & Assessment

- Trace, cut out, and assemble a silhouette
- Assess by displaying silhouettes for students to identify.

Tip

Have the art teacher give students a warm-up lesson in drawing techniques as a prelude to this center.

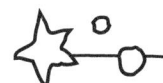

Art   Keepsake Memories, continued

Teacher Materials

- reproducible pages 137 and 138
- projector screen
- adjustable lamp
- table
- stool
- marker

Student Materials

- reproducible pages 137 and 138
- construction paper in a variety of colors
- pencil
- scissors

Teacher Directions

1. Invite parents or grandparents to participate in this activity.
2. Set up and introduce the center.
3. Give each child-adult team a set of reproducibles to complete.

Student Directions

1. Sit on the stool so that your partner can draw a silhouette of your head.
2. When your partner finishes, switch places.
3. It is your turn to draw your partner's silhouette.
4. When you are done, sit at the table together.
5. Cut out the silhouettes.
6. Pick the color of paper you would like to use for your final project.
7. Place the silhouette cutout over the colored paper.
8. Trace the silhouette outline onto the colored paper.
9. Cut it out and glue it in the picture frame on your activity page.

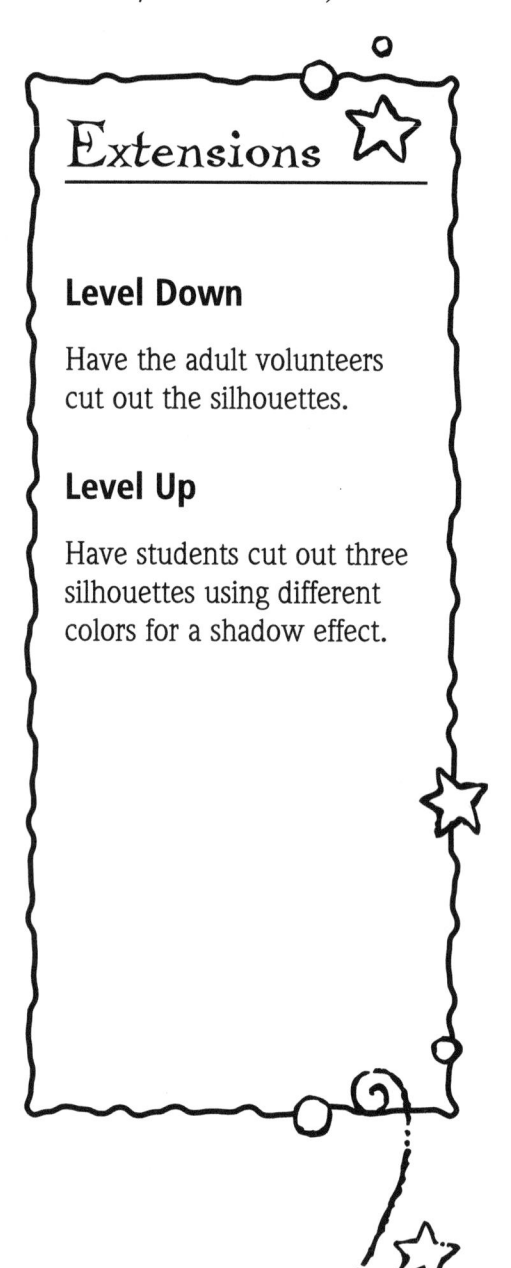

Extensions

Level Down

Have the adult volunteers cut out the silhouettes.

Level Up

Have students cut out three silhouettes using different colors for a shadow effect.

Name _____ Date _____

A Keepsake Silhouette

This is a silhouette of _____

drawn by _____.

Name _____ Date _____

A Keepsake Silhouette

This is a silhouette of _____

drawn by _____.

138

© McGraw-Hill Children's Publishing   0-7682-2941-3 *Learning Center Activities for the New Teacher*

Appendix

The Shopping List

General

CD/tape player with earphones
colored markers
construction paper
crates
easel
envelopes, No. 10
felt
flannel board
freezer paper, white
index cards
manila envelopes, 10" x 12"
paper plates
plastic cups, 8 oz.
self-standing screens
shoe boxes
stuffed animals
tablecloth, disposable
tables, small
tape
tape recorder
wash basin

Language Arts

apple tree
chair, child's
drill
hole punch
napkins
orchard pictures
paper brads
pizza box

plate or tray
plates, luncheon
recordings of poetry and music
ribbon
saucers
teacups
teapot
telephones
utensils
window frame
wood stakes
worktable

Math

24" mailing tube
three-shelf bookcase
apron
balloon bouquet
ballot box
baseball bat
bubble gum
camera
cardboard, 4' x 4'
cloth
coin purse
gold stars, self-adhesive
hook-and-loop fastener stick-ons
ice cream cone
peanuts
pickles
plastic jars, 8 oz.
tomato plant

The Shopping List, continued

Science

bicycle
cardboard tray, 12" x 12"
germ pictures
hard hat
insect pictures
magnifying glass
marsh pictures
microscope
paper towels
photographs of trees
picnic basket
plastic comb
plastic lids
roller-skates
rolling pin
rubber washers
slides, bacteria and viruses
soap
soil samples
tape of nature sounds
thread, lightweight
tissue
tree trunks
tweezers
wool sock
yo-yo

Social Studies

baby bottle
baby doll
bedspread
books
bookshelf
box, playing card size
child's cot or board
corn on the cob, dried
doll crib with blankets
family crest designs
family trees
firewood
globe
lamp, small
mirror, unbreakable
pillow
sticky notes
table lamp
tongue depressors
towels, flour sack
toys
trunk
wash tub, plastic
wooden stakes

Music

bookends
keyboard
tissue paper, white

Art

lamp, adjustable
projector screen
stained glass samples
stool